This b
world o
simple e
after rea
Sue Pag

"What a
The user
manager
developm
Ian Law

"This boo
It is well-
practical v
leadership
the thoug
David Cu

"We have
sustainable
personal e
when each
Iain Napie

Peak Performance Presentations

Peak Performance Presentations

How to present with passion and purpose

Lessons for business from the world of theatre

Richard Olivier and Nicholas Janni

First published in 2004 by
Spiro Press
17–19 Rochester Row
London SW1P 1LA
Telephone: +44 (0)870 400 1000

ISBN 1 84439 097 7

British Library Cataloguing-in-Publication Data.
A catalogue record for this book is available from the British Library.

Library of Congress Cataloging-in-Publication Data on file.

Spiro Press USA
3 Front Street, Suite 331
PO Box 338
Rollinsford NH 03869
USA

Typeset by: JW Arrowsmith Ltd
Printed in Great Britain by: JW Arrowsmith Ltd
Cover images: Carlton (Olivier), Getty Images (Mandela, Churchill and Luther King),
          NBC Universal (Judi Dench)
Cover design by: Cachet Creatives

Spiro Press is part of The Capita Group

Acknowledgements

Richard and Nicholas:

For experimental workshops and professional practice; Wild Dance Events, Flint House, The Findhorn Foundation, Alternatives, The Actor's Centre, The Open Center (New York), The Esalen Institute, The Office for Public Management, The Praxis Centre and the Globe Theatre Education Department. Jacquie Drake, for her visionary ability and nurturing capacity. For deep insight into "Inner Critics" and "Antidotes"; Lowijs Perquin and Al Pesso. For true mastery in Voice; Stewart Pearce. For continued inspiration at every twist and turn – our poet associate William Ayot. For much valued support and friendship along the journey; Ben Walden, Michael Boyle, Yvette Forbes, John Costalas, Mary Mills, Juliet Grayson and all our wonderful team at Olivier Mythodrama. Our publisher, Susannah Lear, whose firm and caring hand steadied our wandering off task, and to Michael Lazarov who willingly suffered extensive redrawing in our attempts to give figurative life to abstract concepts.

Richard:

For putting a notion for theatrical adventure and a spirit for creativity into my blood; my parents, Laurence Olivier and Joan Plowright. For inspiration into the line of Peak Performance; Constantin Stanislavsky, Michael Chekhov and Peter Brook. For what they taught and how they taught it; Professors Michael Hackett, Michael McLean and Tom Orth (UCLA). For full frontal formative theatre experience; Tim Robbins and the Actor's Gang, Mark Rylance and the Globe Theatre. For making it all worthwhile; Shelley, Ali and Troy.

Nicholas:

My first great mentor, Jerzy Grotowski, for his visionary research into authentic performance. Jacques Gardel at Theatre Onze, Lausanne, for three years' transformational actor training. Staff and students at RADA and Mountview Theatre School. All the members of the three incarnations of The Performance Research Project. Kahu AK for the shattering initiation into the Hawaiian Kahuna wisdom tradition. West African master-drummer Adama Drame for allowing me to share your world in Bouake for six months. The Kodo Drummers on Sado island, Japan, for three months of unforgettable power, beauty and exhaustion. Master-drummer Joji Hirota for many Peak Performance concerts together. Roshi John Garrie for body/mind teachings in the Zen tradition. All the ancestors and guardians of the Yoga and meditative traditions that have survived so robustly for so long, and that are such an essential beacon in my life. Margaret Landale, who guided me masterfully through the desolate waters of Beowulf's lake. Jonnie Godfrey, for all the support and encouragement. My children, Leila and Gabriel, for your constant presence and passion, and the inestimable privilege of being your father. And finally, to my wife Hadassa, for a depth of love and partnership I had never dared imagine.

Dedication

To those in all walks of life who carry the flame of authenticity, integrity and inspiration.

To the many brave souls who have entrusted themselves to this work over the years.

To our families, whose love, care and understanding sustain us through the journey.

Prologue

In one of our three-day presentation training programmes, a chief executive began the first morning by delivering a presentation to the group. His intention was to inspire us. He read from a script with a monotonous voice and barely looked up. In short, he bored us.

At the end of three days' intensive work he delivered a final presentation to the group. He began by stepping onto the stage and ceremonially tearing up his original script. He spoke authentically, passionately and with authority. We the audience were spellbound, inspired and moved.

This kind of Peak Performance Presentation is not a special gift for the lucky few, nor is it a trick. It is our natural birthright which skills from theatre can release and enhance.

The process of becoming an excellent presenter is essentially a liberating one. It calls us to overcome our fears and find our true voices. It has been our privilege to share this process with many people over the last few years, and we are delighted to be able to offer you a roadmap for the journey.

Contents

PART 2 – Overcoming the Blocks

PART 3 – Expanding the Repertoire

Introduction

OPENING THOUGHTS

This book is based on two basic beliefs. The first is that all *Presentation is Performance*. The second is that if you are not operating in or near "peak performance" then you are not delivering what you are capable of. We hope you will come to agree with our first belief. If you follow the suggestions and use the tools and techniques in this book you will be able to experience the second for yourself.

When we stand in front of a group to present we enter a different relationship than when we are just talking or taking part in a meeting. The fact that everyone is focused on us creates the type of pressure that performers in all media face. This is why we say that when we are giving a presentation we are performing, and others witness that performance. If we do not recognize this difference we will not use our time with maximum effectiveness.

Presentations are a vital part of successful management and leadership. They do not simply impart information but critically affect how much people trust you, and how far and with what degree of commitment they will follow you. At their best they serve as a medium for inspiration.

Yet in the corporate world, it is our experience that very few people are adequately trained to achieve anything like their full presentation potential, whether this is in front of five, 50 or 500 people. We see two main reasons for this.

First, research has shown that the overall impact of a presentation is determined by three things:

1 How you appear (your energy and confidence);
2 How you sound (the quality, tone and variety of your voice); and
3 What you say (the content).

It may surprise you to know that the relative significance of these is as follows; how you appear counts for 60% of overall impact, how you sound 30%, and what you say only 10%. Yet most people devote at least 90% of their available preparation time to content.

We do not seek to diminish the importance of what you say, but what we do know to be true is that even the most brilliant speech, if delivered in a flat, lifeless way, will have very little impact. This book will help you redress the balance.

"Brilliant Speech"

Secondly, a BBC survey in 2000 found that people's Number One fear – above death, injury or divorce – was public speaking! All but a few of us tend to feel some anxiety when standing at the centre of attention in front of a group of people. This anxiety often severely undermines our delivery. Yet very little effective training is offered to help people manage themselves confidently in this uniquely challenging situation.

Both your authors, Richard Olivier and Nicholas Janni, have spent many years in theatre, directing and training actors to achieve Peak Performance. We have also taught extensively in the field of personal development, helping people to break through the blocks that stood in the way of them achieving personal effectiveness. In 1996 we began combining these methods to offer presentation courses at the Cranfield School of Management in the UK. In 2001 we formed Olivier Mythodrama as a vehicle to take these skills to a broad range of clients. Over the past eight years we have worked with thousands of managers and leaders from many different organizations teaching the tools required for Peak Performance Presentations. This book is a distillation of that process.

THEATRE THEORY

We have both worked at Shakespeare's Globe Theatre in London. That building is at the centre of a renaissance of the theatre world in England. Each age will find its own acting style, and each generation will refine the offering it received from its predecessor. As a theatre student in Los Angeles in the early 1980s, Richard heard a lecture given by the American actor Treat Williams. Williams spoke about the difference between British and American actors: "Basically, the Brits have all the technique but lack the passion, while us Yanks have all the passion but lack the technique." It was, obviously, a generalization, but a useful one nonetheless. Typically, English actors would work from the "outside-in", finding an image for their character and then figuring out how to play it convincingly.

American actors, conversely, would work from the "inside-out", finding a believable personal and emotional connection to the character first and then gradually expanding it to fit the required role.

At the Globe we (and many others) have worked to combine the best of the British with the best of the American – under the inspired guidance of Artistic Director Mark Rylance. Passion *and* Technique, "inside-out" *and* "outside-in" – together they create a tremendous resource.

These same techniques work equally well with managers and leaders as they prepare their business presentations. "Inside-out" is about authenticity, it is about who you are and what you bring to the table. It includes your unique personality and passions. "Outside-in" is about the character you wish to play. It stems from an awareness of the effect you wish to have on your audience, an understanding of the "role requirement" and a knowledge of the techniques that enable you to deliver that role with clarity and conviction.

A truly effective presentation will therefore be a marriage of the two; combining deep inner authenticity with a style that best delivers the desired impact. This is the foundation of Peak Performance.

THE JOURNEY

We offer the reader an experiential journey towards Peak Performance. We know that the techniques explored in this book actually work. They have been refined and distilled from hundreds of years of theatre and personal development practice. If you wish them to make a difference for you, you will need to "rehearse". With practice and application you can make them your own.

In the Introduction we explicate our primary belief – Presentation is Performance. We expand the notion of Peak Performance and offer guidance on how you can best use this book.

In Part 1 we explore the "foundations" of Peak Performance – Presence and Voice. Presence is at the root of effective presenting. If you are not fully Present you cannot truly perform. Some part of you is not engaged. You may be thinking about what has just happened, or worrying about what you will say next, or what else is going on in your busy life. But this transmits itself to your audience, allowing them to disengage from your message. The "Presence" chapter will explore this in detail and teach the fundamentals of relaxation, "grounding" and "arriving" – making sure that you are "there" before you begin. It moves on to suggest a key technique for maintaining presence during a presentation – Dual Attention – being simultaneously aware of what is going on inside you and what is happening outside of you in the room.

The "Voice" chapter introduces you to some simple exercises you can use to expand your vocal range and power. We explain why your voice is such an important part of carrying your message and suggest ways to sustain continued improvement.

Part 2 is "Overcoming the Blocks". Most of us have a very good reason why we do not present at Peak Performance; there is a voice inside our head that gets in our way. We will help you identify this "Inner Critic" and explore the reasons for its existence. In Chapter 4, "The Inner Coach", we take you to the next step where you can learn to "antidote" the negative effect of the Critic with your own internal resources. By learning how to disempower the Critic you will become more confident and assured as you move forward.

Part 3 will enable you to enjoy "Expanding the Repertoire". Most of us have a natural, ingrained style of managing and presenting, which some of us are very good at delivering. However, there is no one style that will suit all presentations. We introduce you to a model drawn from archetypal psychology and allow you to notice your favourite "character". This may be the Good King (Ordering), Great Mother (Nurturing), Medicine Woman (Creating) or Warrior (Asserting). We devote a chapter to each character to allow you to explore their gifts (and weaknesses) in full. Each has something to offer both your preparation and your performance. We offer a range of exercises and activities that will enable you to play each and all of these key characters, as necessary.

Part 4, "Hitting the Mark", prepares you for performance. "Authenticity" (Chapter 10) examines how we can bring ourselves into our presentation to maximize impact. We look at the "masks" we often choose to wear at work and notice how they can inhibit us reaching our audience. We offer exercises to tap into a deeper level of who we really are, and what we really care about. When we can bring authenticity to our work others will sit up and listen.

"Preparing for Peak Performance" extends the notion of effective preparation. We offer practical suggestions to prepare the space you will be presenting into. We condense much of the learning through the book into a simple format for easy assimilation. We suggest a simple sequence of warm-up exercises you can use to prepare yourself for Peak Performance. We walk you from the wings and onto the stage, where the performance begins…

At the end is a list of Further Resources you may wish to explore to embed your learning, or take it further.

The book is illustrated throughout with real-life insights and case studies; many of these are drawn from our own experiences, and the experiences of people with whom we have worked.

Now let's have a closer look at exactly what we mean by Peak Performance.

PEAK PERFORMANCE

Everyone experiences times when they reach a different level of performance. In the theatre we call this "Peak Performance" or being "inspired". In psychology it is referred to as being "in flow", while sports practitioners call it being "in the zone". These experiences occur in all walks of life, and our intention in this book is to enable you to achieve this level of performance more consistently in your business presentations.

Constantin Stanislavsky was one of the most respected teachers of acting of the 20th century. He worked at the Moscow Arts Theatre developing the "inside-out" approach to acting, which was later the source of many modern techniques, including American "Method Acting". He was one of the first modern theatre artists to work on how actors felt as well as what they showed to an audience. He wrote the following to his students:

> "I would like you to feel from the beginning, even if only for short instants, that marvellous feeling that invades you when the creative faculties are working subconsciously and sincerely. You will learn to love this state and to struggle ceaselessly to attain it... it can be compared to the feelings of a prisoner when the chains that had interfered with all his movements for years have at last been removed."
>
> (From *An Actor Prepares*)

This sense of freedom within a structure, whether it be a character on a stage or a presenter at a conference, is an underlying feature of Peak Performance. When we attain this state we produce our best results and also derive great satisfaction from it. It is indeed a "marvellous feeling". Here is how the basketball player Bill Murray describes "the zone":

> "Every so often a Celtic game would heat up so that it became more than a physical or even a mental game, and would be magical. That feeling is very difficult to describe, and I certainly never talked about it when I was playing. When it happened, I could feel my play rise to a new level. It came rarely and would last anywhere from five minutes to a whole quarter or more... It would surround not only me and the other Celtics, but also the players on the other team, even the referees.
>
> At that special level, all sorts of odd things happened. The game would be in a white heat of competition, and yet somehow I wouldn't feel competitive – which is a miracle in itself. The game would move so fast that everything was surprising and yet nothing could surprise me. It was almost as if we were playing in slow motion. During those spells, I could almost sense how the next play would develop and where the next shot would be taken... My premonitions would consistently be correct, and I always felt then that I not only knew all of the Celtics by heart, but also all the opposing players, and that they all knew me... these were the moments when I had chills pulsing up and down my spine."
>
> (From *The Second Wind*)

In both the Arts and Sport such experiences are common. They are often the primary reason why people start on their path, and frequently remain the driving motivation behind the high levels of effort and discipline both fields require. As the jazz pianist Keith Jarrett put it, when speaking of his long-term collaboration with Gary Peacock and Jack De Johnette:

> "I think that Gary and Jack, more and more, we all understand why we're in this trio. It has nothing to do with standard tunes, it has nothing to do with jazz, it has nothing to do with what it seems to be. It has to do with the state of being we are allowed to get in, in front of people."
>
> (From *Keith Jarrett* by Ian Carr)

When we enter the realms of Peak Performance it does feel as if we are elevated to a higher state. Everything becomes heightened, our thinking as much as our senses. We feel more fully alive in such moments. In an interview, Mark Rylance, one of the great modern classical actors, referred to it as "a beautiful experience", and went on to say:

> "The experience is one of losing myself, at least my normal everyday self, and being part of something bigger, and a big part of it is that the spirit of the piece really comes alive – I am out of the way, and it is shining through me. It feels like being graced, and I feel deeply Present. It is something that draws me relentlessly in my work."

Many of us have experienced presentations where we felt "in flow", even if briefly; where there was an effortless feeling of energy and concentration. When a presentation is imbued with this aliveness it achieves a powerful level of impact. In talking with hundreds of managers over the last five years, we have found that everyone without exception has their own version of being "in the zone", if not at work then outside work. It may happen doing a presentation, it may happen in a meeting or when writing a report or designing a new strategy. It may happen when playing golf, when skiing, hiking or playing or listening to music; it may happen when being with the kids. It can happen at any time, in any activity. In his classic study of the subject, *Flow: The Psychology of Optimal Experience*, Mihaly Csikszentmihalyi identified "the zone" as a dimension of human experience that is common to people the world over, regardless of culture, gender, race, age or nationality. At the heart of it is a state of relaxed alertness.

One of the ways we approach the subject in seminars is to ask people to describe the way they feel when they are recognizably in "the zone". What are its various characteristics? The following is a list of the qualities that recur most frequently as people report their experiences. It is always fascinating to see how much congruity there is in different groups, and in different cultures, all over the world. It is very rare for someone to name a quality without everyone else nodding in agreement. See how many of these you recognize from your own experience: *ease, calm, clarity, mastery, balance of alertness/relaxation, flow, confidence, connectedness – to self, to others and to everything around, heightened physical senses, feeling intensely alive, an ability to improvise easily in the moment, altered perception of time, Presence, an expanded sense of self.*

CAN WE CONTROL PEAK PERFORMANCE?

It is important to be clear that "the zone" of Peak Performance is not an either/or scenario. There are degrees to the experience – we can be a bit "in the zone", as it were. Even then our standard of performance will be noticeably higher. The further we go into it, the greater the excellence of our performance, and the deeper the accompanying satisfaction.

The tricky feature of the subject, however, is that while everyone experiences "the zone", at least to some degree, almost no-one knows how or why it occurs, and even less about how to achieve it consistently.

Richard's father, the famous actor Laurence Olivier, was generally regarded as one of the greatest actors of his generation. He was once asked to describe his best performance:

"I was playing *Richard III* and touring Germany in 1946. We were on one of those relentless schedules where we would play in one city one night, travel overnight then set up and play in another city the next day. By the time we got to Hamburg I was exhausted. I sat in my dressing room and fell asleep at the make-up table, not knowing how I would get through that night's performance. At the 'half-hour call' the Stage Manager came in and switched the tannoy system on. As I woke up I could hear the sounds of the audience, mainly from the Armed Services, as they slowly filled the auditorium. As I struggled to pick myself up for the show I became aware of a buzz in the auditorium – I would call it excited expectation. They were here because they wanted to be and they deserved a damn good performance. I don't know how or why, but their expectation lifted me, it gave me access to a level of energy I did not know I had within me. I remember going on stage at the beginning and I remember coming off at the end, but in-between I have very little conscious memory. It was as if I was somehow able to observe myself giving this amazing performance. I recall looking at the audience giving us a standing ovation at the end and thinking; 'How the heck did that happen?' It was extraordinary, a kind of grace that came in, and felt as if it had nothing to do with me."

Nicholas Janni has come to understand "the zone" of Peak Performance.

Nicholas trained actors for 15 years and made the "How" and "Why" the focus of his teaching:

"Since the moments of Peak Performance were so thrilling for both performer and spectator, I was determined to understand how the performer could gain more consistent access to them. In my own development I had practised disciplines such as Yoga, meditation and the Martial Arts, and was studying a number of different forms of self-development as well as undertaking psychological study and training. It gradually became clear that what was asked of the performer was a multi-level approach, conducted with the greatest possible awareness. Peak Performance requires an engagement of all aspects of ourselves – physical, emotional, mental and spiritual. In working all those years with actors, and now with business executives since 1996, I have seen time and again how conscious work in all these realms achieves a level of mastery in performance that many people consider impossible. While no one can guarantee the very highest pinnacles – they are indeed a kind of grace – everyone can move their 'base camp' to a much higher level of consistency and excellence within 'the zone' of Peak Performance. All it takes is awareness, commitment and the right kind of practice."

Peak Performance engages the performer and the audience at all levels. The physical, emotional, mental and spiritual are all active. We often work with one of the greatest modern presentations, Martin Luther King's "I have a dream" speech (quoted in Chapter 8 page 156). Those of you who have watched footage of this speech will recall King's tremendous physical presence and energy, his emotional commitment and expressiveness, his brilliant mental clarity and use of imagery, and the intensity and authenticity of his sense of purpose and service. All the levels are at work.

Peak Performance is a call to engage ourselves more fully. In daily life we tend to compartmentalize everything. We often spend most of the working day in a thinking mode. Then perhaps we work-out or go for a run, so we get physical. Then, if we are not too exhausted, at home we may connect emotionally with friends or family. Some people have a conscious sense of spirit, while others feel really inspired by an event or a person from time to time. Peak Performance Presentations call upon us to integrate these different parts of ourselves, and have them working together and interdependently. It's a high calling, but remember, it's the best feeling in the world, *and* you achieve your best results.

Our central coaching message is very simple: if you are prepared to put in the work, you can do this. You too can become an excellent presenter. With the understanding and the tools we will provide, together with your commitment to practice, you, like the thousands of managers and leaders we have trained, will be able to consistently elevate your presentations to new and powerful levels of impact.

HOW TO USE THIS BOOK

The techniques and exercises in this book form the basis of an extended programme of development of your skills as a presenter. It is a distillation of the 2–3 years' training most actors undergo at drama school, combined with effective techniques for personal development. To get the most from the book will take you somewhere between 3–9 months, working 1–3 hours a week. Much will depend on your time, interest and commitment to practise and learn from the suggested exercises. However, as many people may not have the available time for consistent practice over an extended period, there are several options you might like to consider:

1 You can take one chapter at a time, sequentially, working with it for about two weeks – 10–20 minutes a day or 1–3 hours a week.
2 You can read the whole book, and then go back and work through all the exercises in sequence.

3 You can read the whole book, and then go back and choose the exercises that feel like they have the most relevance to you.

4 You can flick through the chapter and section headings, prioritizing the ones that will be of most use to you, then practise the relevant exercises as and when you have time.

Whichever option works best for you, we encourage you to treat this as a self-managed experiential learning programme. The goal is that you significantly improve your impact and performance level in presentations. The essence of success is practice, supported by reflection. In theatre, the rehearsal process is a time when actors continually try new things out, then step back and consider the results. To get the best out of this book, you too will have to engage in a rehearsal process. You will need to work with the techniques and practise them, in order to embody the learning. Most of the time you will be rehearsing by yourself. Occasionally, you may want to get feedback from a trusted colleague, before or after trying out a new practice in an actual presentation.

In order that you can check on your progress, and to enhance both the practice and the reflection, we recommend that you keep a journal or dedicated notebook. In it you can note what particular practice you are working with at any one time, how you are working with it, what kinds of results you are having, what you might try differently and any other insights related to it. At times we will also be asking you to write in it, and then refer back to what you have written in a subsequent exercise.

We advise you to work with one new practice at a time. Some of them will feel immediately easy, some may take a few days or presentations to get used to. Persevere, and be easy on yourself! When we were kids learning to ride a bike, the best thing to do when we fell off was to get up, dust ourselves down and get back on again with the minimum of fuss (OK, with the occasional hug from mummy/carer). You already practise a number of habits when you give a presentation, whether you are conscious of them or not. They just may not be the most helpful ones. We offer you a new set of habits. Take the time to put each one properly in place.

LEARNING AND PRACTICE

First, a couple of points about learning. In our increasingly "quick fix" culture, paths of genuine development can seem less attractive because of the time and effort they require. We tend to want instant results; but true learning has cycles, and in some parts of the cycle it may look as if we are not progressing. Acquiring any new skill is a process of upward steps and plateaux – it looks like this:

The Learning Cycle

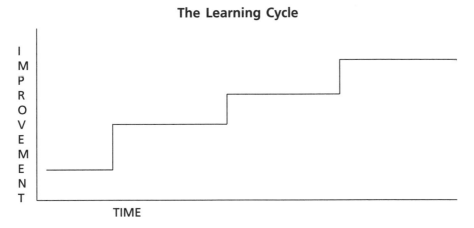

It's very important to know that, in true learning, we spend more time on the plateaux than we do in the phases of exciting and clear upward improvement. But the improvements only happen because of the time spent on the plateaux. These are the times of practice, and more practice, even though you don't seem to be progressing. Many people abandon new learning initiatives when in a plateau phase, because they can't see any apparent improvement. We urge you not to make that mistake. We often use a golf story to emphasize this point. We've heard it ascribed to both Ben Hogan and Jack Nicklaus – we'll go with Hogan:

> Ben Hogan was being interviewed after winning a major tournament. "How is it," the reporter asked, "that under pressure you're able to hit so many miraculous shots?" Hogan answered: "I guess I'm just lucky." "But Mr Hogan," the reporter persisted, "you practise more than any golfer who ever lived. Even when you've won you still go out in the evening and

practise." "Well," Hogan replied, "the thing is, the more I practise, the luckier I get."

In theatre, we found that it is usually the most talented actors who do the longest preparation. England football captain David Beckham is known to put in hours of extra practice on his famous free kicks. That's how it works, there aren't really any short cuts, only practice and more practice, and the deep pleasure of gradually getting better and better.

Both your authors give presentations regularly to a variety of audience sizes, from a board of six people to a conference of a thousand. We keep practising and preparing ourselves for every presentation. The techniques in this book form the foundation of that preparation and they continue to help us slowly and steadily achieve more powerful impact.

DEVELOPING FORESIGHT

Another key is awareness. The more you are aware of what you are doing well, and what you are not doing well, the better. Although for some of us it can be depressing to become aware of areas of incompetence, that is actually the only place from which you can begin to develop competence. We take comfort from the following model of the stages of learning, which suggests four basic positions: Out of Awareness, Hindsight, Midsight and Foresight.

Applied to presentations, the four stages look like this: at Stage 1, "Out of Awareness", we do not know the benefit of a particular practice, so pay no attention to it. At Stage 2, "Hindsight", we have learnt the value of a practice, forget to use it during a presentation, and then realize afterwards. At Stage 3, "Midsight", we realize during the presentation that we are not using the practice, but are not yet fluent enough with it to put it into effect. At Stage 4, "Foresight", we are aware of the need to use the practice during the presentation, and are able to do so.

Let's use an example of a basic performance practice to see how it works. In the chapter on "Presence" we will be introducing you to the importance of breathing correctly while you present. Let's assume that, at the moment, you are at Stage 1, "Out of Awareness". As you progress you will move through the different stages.

The Stages of Learning

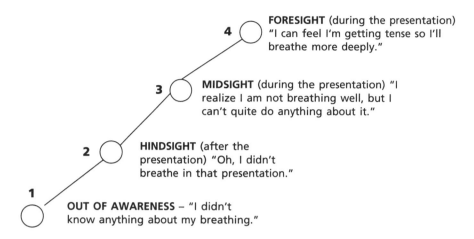

4 FORESIGHT (during the presentation) "I can feel I'm getting tense so I'll breathe more deeply."

3 MIDSIGHT (during the presentation) "I realize I am not breathing well, but I can't quite do anything about it."

2 HINDSIGHT (after the presentation) "Oh, I didn't breathe in that presentation."

1 OUT OF AWARENESS – "I didn't know anything about my breathing."

These are sequential steps, so when you get to Stage 2, "Hindsight" (ie you realize after a presentation that you weren't breathing properly), instead of feeling bad because you "failed", congratulate yourself! You just took an important step towards Stage 3. At Stage 3 you will be able to realize during the presentation that you are not breathing well, though you may not yet be able to change this. In time, and with practice, you move on to Stage 4. Here you are able to realize in the moment that you have restricted your breathing, and can make an immediate correction.

We want to move from Stage 1 to Stage 4 immediately, but this is virtually impossible. You cannot by-pass any of these stages, so remember to give yourself a pat on the back as you move through them!

This book encapsulates many of the most important elements of our working lives. We have had the privilege of working with thousands of managers over the past eight years. Seeing the tremendous changes in their presentations has been a constant source of inspiration to us. We know that as you work through the book you will also start to see the changes occurring. Be patient, and remember – Presentation is Performance – so rehearse, rehearse, rehearse!

We hope you enjoy the journey as much as we have.

Richard Olivier and Nicholas Janni

PART 1

Foundations

Chapter 1

Presence

Presence is the foundation of all good presentations. When a speaker has Presence, they deliver their material with confidence, energy and conviction, and the audience are naturally engaged and receptive. Many people come to work with us believing that Presence is a gift given only to a lucky few. We disagree. We believe that Presence is innate within all of us. It is not a mystery, and it can be developed. Presence is the core of who you are. Have you ever seen a child who does not have Presence?

When you relax, get in tune with yourself and your surroundings, and speak from a feeling of real connection to what you are saying, you too will have Presence. The problem is that most of us are too busy to engage in the simple practices that enable Presence.

How many times have you seen a presenter rush onto the stage, or stand up and start speaking, before they have really settled themselves? In fact, it is common to see people finish their whole presentation before they have really properly started. You just don't feel they were ever really "there".

"Not Arriving"

This has a very unsettling effect on an audience. Some of our clients confess that they "try to get the whole thing over with as quickly as possible"; the trouble is, it shows, all too clearly. If you do not know how to settle properly and feel Present, you will undermine your authority and credibility from the very outset. Relaxed speakers connect easily with their audience. Tense speakers often sound and look as if they are out of control. Lack of voice control, jerky, unsynchronized movements and general restlessness all make an audience feel uneasy.

> Nicholas witnessed a great example of presenting with Presence at a recent conference:
>
> "There were 3,000 people in the audience and the keynote speaker was Daniel Goleman, the famous author/pioneer of 'Emotional Intelligence'. The stage was beautifully lit, and the auditorium was dark. After he was introduced, Goleman walked slowly onto the stage, and stood at the front without saying a word, surveying the audience. After a while he said; 'You know, I really do prefer to see the people I am talking to. Could we please have some light up in the auditorium...' It took a moment or two for this to happen, and then he paused again, before saying 'Great, that's much better, thank you.' And then he started."

Here was a speaker who was unhurried, who took stock of the situation – realized it was not quite to his liking – and did something about it. By the time he started presenting, the audience were relaxed in his presence, and engaged by his humanity, authenticity and openness. He had also shown them that he wanted to give of his best. How often do you allow yourself to settle properly? How often do you feel fully Present, really "there" from start to finish while you are giving a presentation?

Being Present need not take much time or effort, if you have the right foundations. Let's begin by looking at what these foundations are – then we will explore how to practise them.

PRESENT, PAST OR FUTURE?

The most essential requirement of Presence is that you Be Present! Many clients tell us that they spend most of their time during a presentation thinking about what has just happened, or about what might happen next. In other words, they are in the past or the future, not the present. Robert Hastings wrote a great piece called *The Station* that relates to this. He noticed that most people seem to long to arrive at some "station" in the future, when we think everything will be all right, rather than concentrating on living the present moment more fully.

Tucked away in our subconscious is an idyllic vision. We are travelling by train – out the windows, we drink in the passing scenes of children waving at a crossing, cattle grazing on a distant hillside, row upon row of corn and wheat, flatlands and valleys, mountains and rolling hillsides and city skylines.

But uppermost in our minds is the final destination. On a certain day, we will pull into the station. Bands will be playing and flags waving. Once we get there, our dreams will come true and the pieces of our lives will fit together like a completed jigsaw puzzle. Restlessly we pace the aisles, damning the minutes – waiting, waiting, waiting for the station.

"When we reach the station, that will be it!" we cry. "When I'm 18." "When I buy a new Mercedes Benz!" "When I put the last kid through college." "When I have paid off the mortgage!" "When I get a promotion." "When I reach retirement, I shall live happily ever after!" Sooner or later, we realize there is no station, no one place to arrive. The true joy of life is the trip. The station is only a dream. It constantly outdistances us.

"Relish the moment" is a good motto, especially when coupled with Psalm 118:24; "This is the day which the Lord hath made; we will rejoice and be glad in it." It isn't the burdens of today that drive men mad. It is the regrets over yesterday and the fear of tomorrow. Regret and fear are twin thieves who rob us of today.

So stop pacing the aisles and counting the miles. Instead, climb more mountains, eat more ice cream, go barefoot more often, swim more rivers, watch more sunsets, laugh more and cry less. Life must be lived as we go along. The station will come soon enough.

Being Present means you are aware of what is happening inside you, and you are aware of what is happening around you, in the moment in which it is happening. This may sound obvious, but how much of the time are we actually settled in this kind of awareness? Our working life pulls us continually into a flurry of doing, doing, doing, focused on the future or worrying about the past.

"Doing, Doing, Doing"

In this mode we rarely have time to Be Present, attending to the here and now. As *The Station* noted, we often rob ourselves of today and the experience of Now. When we are Present we have a high level of attention to what is happening right here, right now.

This attention opens up something else within our "doing" – we call it the quality of "being". It allows us to feel more connected to ourselves and means we come across very differently to people. In essence, they feel that we are actually there with them, and this alone greatly improves our rapport and impact.

As we become more Present, it usually feels as if we are coming home to ourselves. We are relaxed yet alert. It feels as though we drop into something that is always there, but from which we frequently distance ourselves. Many people say that when they feel Present the world comes into sharper focus. It feels as if they are more awake. This is a good analogy. It also highlights the state of relative sleep within which we may be operating the rest of the time.

THE FOUNDATIONS OF PRESENCE

Over the years we have developed a series of exercises that we call "The Practice of Presence". They will serve to deepen your Presence, and improve your impact in presentations.

It starts with feeling more connected to our bodies. This is a core aspect of the "coming home" feeling. We all knew as children what it was like to inhabit our bodies freely. In our early years all our thoughts and feelings are simultaneously felt in the body. You don't have to show a child how to be physically expressive!

"Free Expression"

As we progressively enter the adult world, however, we learn that the full range and expression of our energy is no longer welcome. We curb our natural flow of emotion and physicality as the environment lets us know that some of it is acceptable and some is not. Each person learns different messages, but the overall pattern is the same. By the time we are adults a significant part of our vitality is forgotten or locked away, and with it much of our natural Presence.

This is reflected directly in our physiology. If we look at young children we see how freely they move, how much energy they have, how loud their voices are. When we start to brace ourselves against the world, and shut down parts of our nature, we do so in two simple ways: we tense our body and we restrict our breathing.

Both these actions are extremely effective ways of closing ourselves down. They also leave us feeling estranged from our own bodies. When we ask people in seminars how much of the time they feel connected to, and at ease in, their bodies during a normal day the average score is rarely higher than 15% of the time. That is the common adult reality. The good news is that, with conscious practice, you can change this.

RELAXATION

The first step is to work with "relaxation". Unless we release some of the tension we carry around with us habitually, and learn to breathe more freely, little else will be possible. We tend to carry so much tension in our body that it becomes our normal experience. We forget it is there. We do not usually become aware of how tense we are until we have a strong experience of relaxation. Then it can be quite a shock to realize just how high our shoulders have been or how much tension we have been carrying in our hips and legs.

Tension is unhealthy and unhelpful in virtually every way you can think of. It blocks our natural energy flow, restricts our vitality and keeps our sensory faculties, our emotions and our thinking processes locked up. It also greatly restricts any chance we have of being physically expressive. It is one of the first things actors have to learn to counteract when they begin their training. Peter Brook, one of the great theatre directors of the 20th century, wrote: "The actor must be trained to become so organically

"Restricted Vitality"

relaxed within himself that he thinks with his body. He becomes one sensitive, responding whole, like the cat. The same is true of the great orchestra conductor. He thinks and transmits as one gesture. The whole of him is one."

A rigid body almost always reflects a rigid mentality, and we waste a tremendous amount of energy maintaining the tension. The famous English "stiff upper lip" (see overleaf) does just what it is intended to do. When you are feeling emotional, one of the simplest ways to block the emotion and any expression of it is to lock your jaw and mouth. The price we pay is increasing numbness to all experience of life – inner and outer.

Once we have worked with relaxation it will be much easier to master the other key parts of "The Practice of Presence" which are Breathing, Grounding and Dual Attention. At this point you have a choice: either you can read through the whole chapter, and then come back to the exercises, or you can do this first exercise in relaxation right now.

"The Stiff Upper Lip"

Some guidelines before you start:

- You can do the exercise reading straight from the book. We will make it clear when to put the book down for a moment.
- You will need about 10 minutes for the first exercise. Make sure you will be undisturbed.
- Find somewhere you can lie down on the floor. You will be more comfortable if you put a couple of medium-sized books under the middle of the back of your head.
- Your body temperature can drop by several degrees when you relax deeply, so make sure you are going to be warm.

- Turn the lighting down or off.
- Have your notebook and pen beside you.

OK, you're ready for an exercise in RELAXATION!

"Relaxation"

Exercise 1a: Relaxation

i) Begin by simply paying attention to how your body feels right now, as you lie on the floor. Notice which parts of it are more in contact with the floor than other parts. Notice whatever sensations there are in different areas of your body. If there is a sensation you would normally call "pain" take your attention right into it. Notice exactly what that sensation feels like.
(Put the book down for a couple of minutes while you do this)
ii) Now pay attention to your breathing, as if you were noticing it for the first time. What does it actually feel like to breathe in and out? Where in your body is there movement as you breathe?
(Book down while you do this)

iii) Take a series of increasingly deep breaths. Let the out breath be an audible sigh. Each time you breathe out, think of letting go, letting go of tension and allowing it to flow out of you into the ground beneath you. Feel your body gently softening, melting each time you breathe out. Notice that you may feel reluctant to breathe out so deeply. A part of you may not want to let go of your tension. That's a normal reaction. Notice it and then see if you can gently ease yourself into deeper and longer out breaths. *(Book down)*

iv) Now let's imagine you are lying on earth, or grass. We speak of Mother Earth, so imagine for a moment that each time you breathe out you are allowing yourself to drop into the welcoming arms of Mother Earth. She accepts you, she embraces you, she welcomes you unconditionally. Allow yourself to savour this unconditionality. At this moment there is absolutely nothing you have to do, nothing you have to be. You are simply welcome. You are safe, you are relaxed, you are open.

(Book down, and lie with your eyes closed until you are ready to end the exercise)

v) Open your eyes and slowly get up. Make some notes about how you feel.

vi) See if you can do this daily for a while. Ten minutes in the morning, or in the evening after work, when you can lie down on the floor and take yourself through this deliberate process of releasing tension.

Through the exercises in this chapter, and the next chapter on "Voice", your awareness of your body will grow substantially. As your awareness develops you will start to notice tension as it happens, and eventually – with Foresight – will be able to relax in the moment. This is of enormous benefit both before and during a presentation. Most clients feel, even after one brief experience of relaxation, much more Present. This is an important first step towards the optimum condition of relaxed alertness. Now let's balance the relaxation with the other three practices – Breathing, Grounding and Dual Attention.

BREATHING

In this section we are going to take the work with breathing a step further.

Working consciously with our breath is one of the simplest and yet most powerful of the tools available to us.

Many paths of self-development, including Yoga, Tai Chi and other Martial Arts, have worked with breathing as a core practice for hundreds of years. Actors, singers, dancers and sports performers all work consciously with their breath. The racing driver Jackie Stewart once said that when he was really "in the zone" he breathed his way through corners. Almost all the managers we have ever worked with report that working deliberately with breathing opens up new levels of energy and Presence.

As we saw earlier, restricting our breathing is one of the main ways we shut down our whole system. Most adults breathe shallowly in their upper chests. If you observe yourself, you will also notice that the moment you come under any stress you probably stop breathing altogether for a few seconds. Our "normal" breathing habits are every bit as unhelpful as unnecessary tension.

Dennis Lewis, author and international teacher of mind/body approaches to healing and self-development, wrote in his book *The Tao of Natural Breathing*:

"Our chronic shallow breathing reduces the working capacity of our respiratory system to only about one third of its potential, diminishes the exchange of gases and thus the production of energy in our cells, deprives us of the many healthful actions that breathing naturally would have on our inner organs, cuts us off from our own real feelings and promotes disharmony and 'dis-ease' at every level of our lives... There is also absolutely no doubt that superficial breathing ensures a superficial experience of ourselves."

The habit of shallow breathing is deeply ingrained, but all it takes to change it is consistent practice. In the "breathing" exercise below your body will have the opportunity to settle back into the way it is designed to breathe. This will be wide and deep in your torso. It is the natural breath that you see in children and in animals – it is how you breathe when you are asleep, and not interfering!

It is helpful to include the "breathing" exercise after the relaxation, when you have time. If you do it on its own, the same suggestions apply:

- You can do the exercise straight from the book. We will make clear when to put the book down for a moment.
- You will need about 10 minutes for the exercise. Make sure you will be undisturbed.
- Find somewhere you can lie down on the floor. You will be more comfortable if you put a couple of medium-sized books under your head.
- Your body temperature can drop by several degrees when you relax deeply, so make sure you are going to be warm.
- Turn the lighting down or off.
- Have your notebook and pen beside you.

Exercise1b: Breathing

i) Bring your feet up towards your bottom, place them parallel, and about the width of your hips apart. Place your hands on your stomach, finger tips not quite touching. When you breathe naturally, there is movement in the chest, but more significantly, there is also movement in your stomach. As you breathe in this whole area should expand, pushing your hands up. As you breathe out, the opposite should happen – this area subsides and your hands drop down.

You can start to make this happen by gently pushing down as you breathe out. As you breathe out, relax and let go, as in the "relaxation" exercise. At the end of the out breath, feel the need to breathe and ALLOW the in breath to happen without effort or interference on your part. This is one of the biggest keys. Don't do it, let it happen. You will feel quite a dynamic quality to the in breath once you release it in this way, and you will feel muscles that you are perhaps not used to spring into action.

(Book down while you let your body settle into this)

ii) Keep exploring this: emptying and relaxing on the out breath, "allowing" the in breath. You will feel your breath settle into this stomach area, and you will also feel the breath widening, meaning that the palms of your hands will feel the side of your stomach expanding, and you will feel your lower back also pushing down into the floor as you breathe in. Keep relaxing, keep allowing... As you do this you should find that you can gently lengthen the out breath. The in breath needn't be longer than a count of four, the out breath can be five, seven, 10, 12... work with this. Try to get to 20. You'll be surprised to see how long the out breath can be as you relax more and more. Feel these tidal waves of breath. They are moving through the very centre of your being, irradiating the area of your body that the Martial Arts consider to be the centre of your power and vitality.

(Book down while you work to lengthen the out breath)

iii) When you are ready, have a good slow stretch. Stretch as you breathe. Notice how much more sensitized you are to your body. Enjoy the stretching the way a cat does.

(Book down while you stretch)

iv) Now slowly bring yourself up to sitting. Keep your eyes closed. Sit in whatever way is comfortable for you. Once you are settled, let your breathing drop into the same mode as when you were lying down. Notice how you can use exactly the same process of relaxing and allowing to achieve the same depth and width of breathing. This is essential. It is what you will need to do when you are standing in front of an audience.

v) Make some notes about how it felt to breathe in this way.

vi) Once you have done this enough times to feel that your body understands it, you should incorporate this into everyday life. Find the best times to focus on it. Perhaps when you are driving, perhaps when you are sitting in front of your computer screen or walking. You might want to put little notes around the place, and on your computer screen, to remind you. Basically, practice this as much as you can, so that it gradually becomes second nature. Breathe more fully throughout the day, and become more aware of the times when you almost stop breathing. It will be one of the most valuable things you can do.

GROUNDING

From the outside, someone who is "grounded" looks and feels as if they are really there, as if they are standing their ground confidently. From the inside, when you are grounded you feel strong, solid and supported. You feel as if you have the right to be there.

Tension has the effect of lifting us away from the sensation of connection with the earth. It is this connection that gives us the experience of being grounded; the following exercise will help you to feel it.

Exercise 1c: Grounding

You should do both "grounding" exercises standing. Each lasts no more than five minutes. Read through the instructions before each one.

i) Stand with your feet shoulder width apart and parallel. Balance the weight evenly between the front and the back of your foot. Make sure your knees are relaxed. We block our energy by bracing our knees. Start to push your feet into the ground, gently and slowly at first. Gradually increase the speed and firmness of the contact. If it helps, imagine that you have roots coming out from the sole of your foot. They go down through the floor, through the foundations of the building and down into the earth below.

You can do this any time you want without anybody noticing. It is essential before a presentation, and very useful during it. As you begin to feel more grounded, the lower half of your body, from the waist down, will feel more powerful. This is your support, your foundation. As it grows in strength your upper body will be able to rest, straight yet relaxed, on this very solid base.

The second step of opening this quality is to let your weight drop, so that your legs start to support you in the way they were designed to.

Exercise 1c: Grounding (cont'd)

ii) Stand as before and then, on an out breath, let your knees buckle so your torso drops down a foot or so. Your head can gently slump forward. Feel the full weight of your body. On an out breath, slowly come up by pushing your feet down into the ground. Stand strong and upright now. Feet planted, knees relaxed, weight dropped, spine free and straight. Feel the natural power and grace of this position, and let your breath flow strongly again through the belly and chest, as it did when you were lying down in the "breathing" exercise. If you need to, take a deep breath to let go of any unnecessary tension that may have built up. Repeat.

iii) Make some notes on how it feels to be more grounded.

Breathing and Grounding are the physical foundations of Presence. Practise them as much as you can in everyday life so they become new habits, and regularly available to you when you present.

DUAL ATTENTION

The last practice, Dual Attention, is the tool that will most powerfully hold you in a state of Presence during your presentations. Simply, Dual Attention means being aware of the inner and the outer at the same time. You notice what is happening inside you, and you notice what is happening around you. In daily life we are very rarely in this balance. Sometimes we are lost in our interior world; when we are thinking hard about something this can be perfectly appropriate. But when we are dealing with the outside world we mostly get pulled out of ourselves much too easily, meaning that we lose self-awareness. Our attention gets focused too much in the exterior reality, and when that happens we are automatically less Present. Being Present means being fully aware of yourself and the world at the same time!

Exercise 1d: Dual Attention

i) Right now, as you read this, become more aware of yourself. Become aware of your body, pay attention to your breathing and to the sensation of your contact with your chair and the ground.
(Now read the instructions for the rest of the exercise, so that you can put the book down)
ii) Accentuate this by closing your eyes for a moment. Take a deep breath and pay attention to breathing, to your feet touching the ground, to your overall body feeling. Focus all your attention inwards. Now, hear some of the sounds that are around. Let them simply be there, as part of your overall

"Dual Attention"

attention. Keep noticing your internal world of sensation at the same time. Now imagine that in a moment you are going to open your eyes and look out into the world. But at the same time you are going to remain just as aware of yourself as you are now. Make a clear picture in your mind of how that will be. It will help if, when you open your eyes, you think of the world outside you as coming towards you, rather than you going out towards it. **iii)** When you are ready, open your eyes. Look at the ground in front of you first, while you stabilize the Dual Attention, inner and outer at the same time. When you are ready, raise your eye level so you are looking at the world around you. At the same time as you look at the world, remain aware of your breathing, of your contact with floor and chair, of your body as a whole. Notice how this feels.

As with the other practices, you should aim to work with this as often as possible in your everyday life. The practice starts in a simple way by using your physical body as the object of your self-awareness. Whenever you remember, pay attention to the sensation of breathing, notice the contact of your feet with the ground. Aim to keep this inner awareness in place whatever else you are doing. As this settles and becomes more constant, you will start to become more attuned to other dimensions of your inner world. You will notice more subtle physical sensations, you will notice shades of feeling as they rise and pass, and you will notice the rich stream of thoughts, associations and memories passing through the screen of your mind. You will do all of this while paying equal attention to the world around you. All it takes is practice.

Think of it as a 50–50 split. 50% of your attention is within yourself, 50% goes out in to the world. It is like the double-headed indicator arrow in your car:

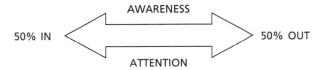

At first you might suppose this will make you less effective, because it looks like you will not be giving your full attention to what you are doing, or whomever you are with. Actually, the opposite is true. You will perform much better, because you will feel much more Present. But the proof is in the pudding. Practise it and you will see the difference.

> A senior bank executive on one of our programmes was called to an urgent lunch meeting on the second day of the programme. As always, we had been working with this practice. When he returned he told us how he had practised Dual Attention during the meeting. His observation was that this caused him to be much more Present. This meant he had also listened much better than usual. Although he had known the person he was meeting for some time, he was struck by how this had become the best and most authentic conversation they had ever had. He had no doubt that his state of Presence was the main reason for this.

By now you are probably beginning to see the interdependency of all of this, and how natural the interconnection between mind and body is. As you de-contract physically, so your experience of yourself and the world around you comes more alive. Dual Attention holds it all in place.

During a presentation, Dual Attention will give you crucial new levels of awareness and choice. First you will be much more aware of what is going on out there in your audience, and how you might need to adapt to that. (In Part 3, "Expanding the Repertoire", we will be giving you a wide range of options for this adaptation.) Secondly, you will be far more attuned to different lines of thought within yourself, and be able to select whichever is most appropriate at that time. You will also be more confident about improvising in the moment, without losing track of where you are in your overall structure. Lastly, you will notice when unnecessary tension is developing in you, and be able to correct it; you will keep your breathing full and deep, and you will remember to keep grounding yourself.

The practice of Dual Attention will help you develop what we call a "witness" or "pilot" part of your consciousness. This part will always be looking on and assessing constructively. In acting, this is regarded as one of the symptoms of Peak Performance. Mark Rylance comments: "I feel highly present, awake and aware in those times, a consciousness that does not cling to anything around, and has no self-consciousness about it. My radar is also incredibly finely tuned, and I have an extraordinary sense of what is about to happen. I instinctively make the right choices, and these lead me in good directions."

Notice that this awareness is quite different from self-consciousness. The latter makes you feel uncomfortable because it always contains some kind of judgement, and what we will later refer to as an "Inner Critic". The awareness within Dual Attention makes only a positive contribution. The great Russian acting teacher Michael Chekhov spoke of how in Peak Performance the actor's "everyday I" gives way to a higher "I" or self. This is another way of naming the inner "pilot" or "witness" we awaken through Dual Attention. In his book, *To the Actor*, Chekhov remarks:

"You will recall that with the experience of this new 'I' you felt first of all an influx of power rarely experienced in your routine life. This power permeated your whole being, radiated from you into your surroundings... thanks to this power, you are able to feel to a high degree your real presence on stage. This 'higher self' has the building material well in hand; it begins to mould it from within and increases your inner activity. In short, it puts you in a creative state."

Exercise 1e: Practising Dual Attention in Everyday Life

i) Practise Dual Attention as much as possible until it becomes second nature. Catch yourself during a conversation with someone, and re-focus your inner attention. Do this over and over, as many times as you can each day. Ask yourself: "Am I in 50-50 or 60-40 or 70-30 or..?"

We both know how crucial all these practices are to the success of each presentation we give. Now an insight from Nicholas:

"Settling into a feeling of being Present, both before and during a presentation, has become an essential aspect of how I work. It allows me to feel really comfortable in front of an audience, and from that follows the ability to make humorous and serious rapport with equal fluidity. I can sense their mood, and what energy I need to bring to my material. My ease puts them at ease, and generates natural receptivity. This is a winning formula!

Being able to settle into that Presence has largely been a question of doing exactly what we are encouraging you to do: practise, practise, practise. The more I practise it, the better I get at it. It also requires me each time to do the necessary inner work, 'The Practice of Presence'. Every so often I get a timely reminder of what happens if I am less than rigorous in my preparation. Basically, I just don't completely hit the mark, and although my performance will still be perfectly decent, it will not meet the high standards I have come to expect of myself.

Presence, being Present, is without a shadow of a doubt the core ground out of which my best performances arise, whether I am working with a group of six people or addressing a thousand delegates at a conference. And I know for certain that being Present is almost entirely within my control. It is down to me."

EVERYDAY PRACTICE

The key to developing Presence in your presentations is to work at it as much as you can on a daily basis, in less stressful situations. Most people find that the problem does not lie in actually doing each practice – they are quite simple in themselves. The problem lies in remembering to do them! So treat this as an opportunity to get creative about how you remind yourself. Here are some suggestions:

- Post-it Notes around the place are a good start. Put one on your computer screen that says "Breathe!" or "Dual Attention". Try putting one on your car windscreen and at various places around your home.
- Make little cards that you can carry around in your pocket. Each day put one card in your pocket; use it to remind yourself of the practice you want to work with during the day.
- Each time the phone rings let it be a trigger. First ring, take a deep breath, second ring, focus your inner attention, then pick the phone up.
- Use going through doorways as a reminder. Each time you go through a door, remember to take a deep breath and be aware of your feet in contact with the ground.
- During conversations, pay attention to your breathing and to your feet contacting the ground, even if you are sitting.
- Any time you are walking, even a short distance, use this as an opportunity to practise being grounded. Pay attention to placing your feet on the ground. Pay attention to the overall sensation of moving.
- Buy a new pen, and each day let it represent one practice you want to work with. Wherever you go at work, put the pen down on a desk/table where you can see it, so it reminds you of the practice.

In short, use everyday activities and situations as an opportunity. Use your notebook to keep track of which practice you are working with, how you are doing it and what results you are getting. Be light yet firm with yourself. Consistent practice is the key.

Opposite is an example of using an everyday activity like driving as an opportunity to practise Presence. It is adapted from an exercise in a book called *Mastery* by George Leonard, one of America's leading pioneers in the field of mind/body development.

Exercise 1f: Driving as High Art

Say you need to drive 10 miles to work. You might consider the trip itself as in-between time, something to get over with. Or you could take it as an opportunity for the "Practice of Presence". In that case:

i) You would approach your car in a state of full awareness, conscious of the time of day, the temperature, the wind speed and direction, the angle of the sun or the presence of rain, snow or sleet. Let this awareness extend to your own mental, physical and emotional condition.

ii) Take a moment to walk around the car and check its external condition, especially the tyres. Make sure the windscreen and windows are clean enough to provide good visibility.

iii) Open the door and get into the driver's seat. Fasten the seatbelt, check the rear-view mirror. Then, before starting the engine, relax and take a deep breath. Pay special attention to releasing any tension you may have in your neck and shoulders. Lean back so that your back makes firm contact with the seat. Become aware of the pressure of your buttocks and legs on the seat itself; feel yourself merging with the seat, becoming one with the entire car.

iv) Start the engine and attend carefully to its sounds and vibrations. Check all of the gauges; make sure there is plenty of fuel.

v) Taking this short trip will afford you many opportunities for practice. These are a few of the particularly exquisite skills offered every driver: anticipating the possible moves of all the cars in your field of action; entering a curve at the correct speed and accelerating slightly during the turn; braking smoothly and with a feeling of continuity rather than rushing up behind another car and slamming on the brakes; engaging the clutch with perfect synchrony; changing lanes without discomforting other drivers; dealing gracefully with the unexpected.

In our seminars, dramatic changes occur as delegates settle into the foundation of their natural Presence. Everyone watching sees and feels the transformation. Their presentations have so much more impact, they are so much more engaging. The person is "there", inhabiting and embodying their words, and it makes all the difference in the world.

Chapter 2

Voice

The sound of our voice plays a crucial role in how we come across in presentations. Depending on its quality, it can attract or repel people very quickly. This goes far beyond what we are actually saying – it is a visceral, instinctive reaction on the part of the audience. We often form a core impression within seconds of hearing somebody speak. Think of how quickly you assess someone you have not met when you hear them on the telephone. When a person's voice is warm and open we are automatically drawn to them. Many public figures know this, and have coaching to improve their voice.

In this chapter we want to help you develop the quality of your voice. While some older styles of speech and elocution training aim to create an artificially "good" voice, our approach is to liberate your natural voice. Kristin Linklater, one of the performing world's most respected voice coaches, puts it like this:

> "The objective is a voice in direct contact with emotional impulse, shaped by the intellect but not inhibited by it. Such a voice is a built-in attribute of the body, with an innate potential for a wide pitch range, intricate harmonics and kaleidoscopic textural qualities. The natural voice is transparent – revealing, not describing, inner impulses of emotion and thought. The person is heard, not the person's voice."

> (From *Freeing the Natural Voice*)

We have often been struck by how, whenever someone starts talking about something they genuinely care about, their voice can change quite dramatically. If it was flat and dull before, suddenly it becomes warm and expressive. Their "habitual" voice gives way to their "natural" voice. As Patsy Rodenburg, Head of Voice at the UK's Royal National Theatre, says:

"A good note to any public speaker is always 'If it matters to you, it will matter to us'."

We will explain the techniques that will enable you consistently to access the richness and expressiveness of your natural voice. The vocal tradition of the English theatre is admired the world over. We have had the privilege of working with several exceptional voice coaches, including Stewart Pearce, Master of Voice at Shakespeare's Globe. The material in this chapter is drawn from their expertise as well as from our experience in theatre practice and training.

BASIC PRINCIPLES

Our voice is a physical instrument. The sound of the voice is generated by physical processes, so any unnecessary tension in our body will have an immediate effect on the voice. In the chapter on "Presence" you worked to relax, and then feel more in contact with your body. In this chapter we will be taking that work further. Whatever restrictions or limitations you may have in regard to your voice, these are almost all the result of inappropriate tension. When you speak with an open and free sound, we really hear *you*, which, of course, is the whole point.

Tension originates in our emotional and psychological self, as well as in our physical self. Some tension results from bad physical habits and daily stress, some of it goes deeper. The English "stiff upper lip" for example, mentioned in the last chapter, is underpinned by opinions and fears about emotion. The tension in that lip keeps the natural flow of emotion under lock and key. Hardly surprising, then, that it will also negatively affect our voice. However, almost all the work in this chapter is entirely physical, and the physical approach alone will make a very big difference. If you discover along the way that you make some internal judgements about increasing your range of vocal expression there may be some psychological tensions affecting your voice too. Make a note of them, and we will address them fully in the next Part of the book, "Overcoming the Blocks".

Tension means that many people's habitual voice – the voice they speak with every day – is several notes higher in pitch than their natural voice. Tension will also thin the voice out and restrict its natural resonance. When you are presenting well, intellect and emotion, body and voice work in harmony. The foundation for this is breath moving freely in your body. When your voice is open, your breath will be coming from the lowest possible point in your body, the pelvis area, then moving up through the stomach, chest, throat, then out of your mouth. This will also activate the three main vocal resonators in your body – the head, chest and stomach.

Most of the time, particularly in the work environment, we end up using the head resonator exclusively. This is mainly the result of spending so much time thinking and communicating data, and not expressing emotion at work. Data is dry and flat, and often speakers communicate data in a dry and flat way – which doesn't serve them or their audience well. Unless we work consciously to loosen the voice and employ all three resonators appropriately, our voices lose tone and impact. We become talking heads, cut off at the neck. This is often the key difference between speakers we enjoy listening to and those we have difficulty sustaining our attention for. These voices carry no feeling. We have all heard them at conferences – actually, usually we only hear the first five minutes and then nod off!

Actors can also miss the mark in this way. Some concentrate on thinking through their part rather than feeling it. If you go to the theatre often you will know that some actors just don't hold your attention. We often find that these actors are not using resonators effectively, and therefore not enabling their voices to carry the feeling of the words.

The moment you use your chest resonator (as well as the head resonator) the whole timbre and quality of your voice changes. It drops a couple of notes and sounds warmer and richer. Most importantly, the sound produced by the combination of head and chest resonators carries a rich mix of feeling and thought. It is much more likely to reach people's hearts as well as their minds. It sounds like *you*. (Because people get so used to their habitual voice, when they first hear their natural voice they often feel it sounds unnatural, until they practise and get used to it.)

The third resonator, the stomach, creates a powerful low sound. It carries a feeling of deep melancholy, and it can also be extremely seductive (think Barry White). You will rarely use this resonator on its own, however, when it is open it adds another layer of resonance to your voice. In peak moments of presentation, all three resonators will be active, and it will feel as if your whole body is contributing to the sound.

So let's take a look at how the "open" voice works, and then suggest physical exercises for you to practise.

PREPARING THE BODY

You will be standing up for the next sequence of exercises. Remember to stand in a grounded way, with your knees relaxed. The effectiveness of any physical warm-up is reduced by about 90% if we do it on a held breath, so make sure you breathe easily through each exercise. Let your body take a deep breath whenever it wants to.

THE HEAD

The head should sit balanced on top of the spine, like a ping-pong ball balanced on a spout of water. It can turn and go up and down with the minimum of effort. If you feel this it will give you a natural feeling of weightlessness in your head, and some of the unnecessary tensions will drop away. Your head becomes lighter and freer. Unnecessary facial tension can also affect your sound, so you need to become aware of unnecessary frowning and lifting of the forehead.

Exercise 2a: Aligning the Head

i) Imagine a ping-pong ball balanced on a spout of water. Let your head become like the ball. Make some very small movements to help you find the point of effortless balance. Make sure your head is neither jutting forward nor pushed back. Settle into the sensation of your head floating in this way. Your neck should feel slightly elongated. Swallowing should be really easy, and you are now looking out at the point of the horizon, neither above nor below it.

ii) Stretch your face wide. Make the biggest "startled" expression you can, then relax your face. Repeat.

iii) Now make some smaller movements, like raising your eyebrows, then your forehead. Each time, settle back into a neutral face. Discover what the relaxed face feels like, and remember it.

iv) Feel the weight of your head by letting it drop onto your chest. Move the head gently and slowly from side to side. If it feels comfortable to do so, take this into a full roll. Be slow and careful. Don't force it. When your head is tilted back, move it slowly from side to side. Come back to neutral. The ping-pong ball on a spout of water.

THE SHOULDERS

The shoulders should also feel free and floating like the head. Mostly, our shoulders are up, and this restricts our breathing, which in turn affects our voice. Tense shoulders can also be the source of headaches and neck and shoulder pain.

Exercise 2b: Freeing the Shoulders

i) Breathe in and raise your shoulders as high as they will go. Hold for a moment. As you breathe out let them drop down to a natural position. Don't force them down. See if you can let their weight cause the drop rather than you doing it. Repeat a couple of times.

ii) Now start to circle each shoulder in turn in its socket. Work them firmly but gently. Don't be alarmed if you hear some crunching sounds. Circle forwards and backwards till they feel looser. They should feel free and light.

iii) Now start to swing each arm in turn, forwards and backwards. Let the weight of the arm do the work. Keep the movement fluid, not jerky. Then go through 360° with each arm, and let it come to a natural rest.

THE JAW

As with the shoulders, jaw tension can easily become habitual, and we then cease to notice it. When relaxed the jaw should open easily, otherwise words get clenched in the mouth and cannot come out clearly. The teeth shouldn't touch, even though the lips are together. Tension at the back of the tongue can also muffle sound.

Exercise 2c: Loosening the Jaw

i) Begin by massaging your face all over. Use your fingers, and also the palms of your hands. Move all the different parts separately – cheeks, mouth, lips, ears, nose, forehead.

ii) Gently stretch the mouth open wide, then release it. Repeat this several times.

iii) Chew. Circulate the jaw in chewing motions. Always be gentle with the jaw. If you suffer from jaw tension, repeat this chewing motion during the day.

iv) Finally, stretch the tongue. Open your mouth wide, though without any feeling of strain, and put your tongue right out. Try to extend it, without overdoing it.

THE SOFT PALATE

Not something we normally think about, but a hot topic for voice teachers! If you run your tongue back in the top of your mouth you feel a hard palate in the roof of your mouth. Further back, you find a softer flap that moves. This is your soft palate. Its function is to separate the nasal cavity from the mouth. When it is not working properly your voice sounds nasal, and words are less clearly articulated. It is quite simple to exercise your soft palate.

Exercise 2d: The Soft Palate

i) Brace the tip of your tongue behind your bottom teeth. Keep the jaw relaxed, and make the sounds "k" and "g". Repeat them quite quickly – it will sound as if you are gagged. This will quickly and effectively loosen the soft palate.

THE SPINE

The spine is the core structure of the body, and many physical disciplines the world over focus on its correct alignment. The spine should be proud and erect, yet not rigid. The vertebrae of the spine should stack evenly on top of each other. Too rigid and you cut off your breath, too loose and you cut off support and energy. Below are some good ways to work with the spine.

Exercise 2e: Loosening the Spine

i) Gently start to wriggle the spine. Make the movements as undulating as you can, as if you were a belly dancer. Allow your head and shoulders to follow the movement, but keep your main focus on the spine. Remember to breathe freely while doing this.

ii) Focus on the centre of your chest and circulate it in as big a circle as you can. Now push it right back, then right forward. Breathe freely.

The following exercise takes a little longer, but is one of best ways of working with the spine. Read the instructions through before you do it.

Exercise 2f: Aligning the Spine

i) If your spine is strong, from a standing position start to very slowly tilt your head forward. Think of each vertebra in the neck moving forward, one at a time. Very slowly extend this down into the spine. As each vertebra moves forward, so your spine starts to bend forward. Continue really slowly until you are fully bent over, with your knees bent and your arms hanging down (see illustration below). Make sure your head and neck are relaxed.

If someone were to touch your head they should be able to move it easily.

Now you are going to reverse the process. Starting from the very bottom vertebra of your spine, bring each one back up, and as you do so, bring your spine back up one step at a time. Do this as slowly as you can. When your spine is straight, your head will still be bent forward, so the final step is to bring the neck slowly into upright alignment. Keep your knees relaxed. Breathe freely.

If you feel your spine is weak, try the exercise below.

Exercise 2g: Strengthening the Spine

i) Sit upright, at the edge of a solid chair (see illustration below). Keeping upright, move about gently, so you can experience your upright spine in motion. Be aware of the base of your spine, how it supports the upright spine. Rock gently back and forward. Still seated, gently undulate your spine, then return to the upright position.

If you spend a lot of the day sitting down, you should try and do as many of the spine exercises as you can – several times a day. Pay attention to your posture as much as possible while sitting. Try not to slump. You'll improve your resonator access and save yourself a lot of back pain at the same time.

BREATH

Proper breathing is the foundation of all successful voice work, so we need to look in more detail at the process and apparatus of breathing. In the chapter on "Presence" we introduced you to the practice of deeper breathing, rooted in the abdomen. Let's notice what happens to the body during this practice.

As you breathe in, your lungs fill and expand at the sides. The back and front of your ribcage open – in particular the two lower ribs, the "floating ribs", which are not attached at the front. Your diaphragm moves down and out and the abdominal muscles release (what we referred to as pushing your hands up in the previous work). When you are deeply relaxed, or breathing hard after exertion, you can feel this movement go right down into the lower abdomen.

When you exhale all the above processes are reversed. The muscles move in together. If you exhale all the way out right now you will feel this happening. The exiting air is what fills and sustains the voice as we speak. All kinds of problems arise when there is not enough of it!

Exercise 2h: Resonator Breathing

Remember, there should be no movement in the shoulders or upper chest when you breathe in. If you rise up in this area you prevent air from going down into the lungs. The in breath should be as effortless as possible. Relax, and let it happen.

i) Place the palms of your hand on the side of your torso, just below your ribcage. Breathe out, relax, feel the need to breathe, and allow your body to take a big in breath. Feel the expansion of your ribcage. Feel it contract as you breathe out. Repeat several times.

ii) Now place your hands on your stomach, and repeat. Feel the expansion of your stomach as you breathe in. Feel it contract as you breathe out. Try it with bigger breaths, always making sure that you do not lift your shoulders. Keep breathing like this for a couple of minutes – see how you can become more and more grounded if you breathe in this way, how the in breath can take you downwards rather than upwards, and how effortlessly you can fill your lungs with air. This is how you need to breathe when in full flow during your presentations.

Now the body is ready we can move on to the voice. We will start with pure sound itself, then work with words and text.

MAKING SOUND – FIRST STEPS

The first step is to find an open and relaxed sound.

Exercise 2i: Making Sound

This exercise will take about 10 minutes. You will need to lie on the floor. Put a couple of books under your head, and have your feet close up to your buttocks, flat on the floor, the width of your hips apart, knees pointing upwards (see illustration below).

i) Take some deep breaths, and use the out breath to let go of tension. Settle your breathing so it is wide and deep.
ii) Keeping the mouth and jaw relaxed, on the next out breath make the sound "zzzzzzz", counting to 10 on your fingers. Repeat three times, each time lengthening the out breath 12–15–20.

iii) Now use the sound "sssssss", counting to 10 on your fingers. Repeat three times, each time lengthening the out breath 12–15–20.

iv) Now make the sound "haw". Relax as you make the sound so it resonates deep down in your chest and stomach, counting to 10 on your fingers. Repeat three times, each time lengthening the out breath 12–15–20.

v) Now make the sound "hoo". Focus the sound in your chest, counting to 10 on your fingers. Repeat three times, each time lengthening the out breath 12–15–20.

vi) Now make the sound "how". Focus the sound in your throat, counting to 10 on your fingers. Repeat three times, each time lengthening the out breath 12–15–20.

vii) Now make the sound "hee". Focus the sound in the centre of your head, counting to 10 on your fingers. Repeat three times, each time lengthening the out breath 12–15–20.

viii) Now imagine you have lips in the centre of your chest, and let them make a "Ha" sound. Repeat. This sound will be your voice at its most natural. Repeat several times.

ix) Finish by making an "mmmmm" sound, and feel the vibration throughout your body.

Now your voice should be "warmed up", it is time to put it to use. The next exercise is recommended as an immediate follow on to the previous one.

Exercise 2j: Sounding Words

i) Sit in a chair. Keep your spine straight, either by sitting forward on the edge of the chair, or by pushing the base of your spine into the back of the chair so the rest of your spine can keep straight. (Remember, never lift your shoulders as you breathe in. The in breath pushes your stomach and ribcage out. There should be no movement in your shoulders.)

ii) After the final "mmmmm" sound in Exercise 2i, using exactly the same sound, on your next out breath say, "Good morning, my name is..."

iii) Try the same thing with "Tiger, tiger, burning bright, in the forests of the night". Make sure you are not reverting to your habitual voice, which will be higher in pitch than the "mmmmm" sound.

iv) Try it with "O for a muse of fire, that would ascend the brightest heaven of invention".

Keep practising until you get a clear understanding of speaking with your natural note, with both head and chest resonators contributing. This takes less effort than you think. All you have to do is let yourself "sit" in the sound. Get used to what this sound sounds and feels like. Keep returning to it as often as you can, however briefly, just by humming the "mmmmm", then speaking a sentence, in the car, in the bath…

It may take you a while to really trust this, just as it does for actors at the beginning of drama school. Whenever you move away from this sound it will normally be because you are using unnecessary effort, and therefore creating tension in your body. One symptom of this would be raising your forehead as you speak. You will also hear your voice clearly rising in pitch.

Here is another good way to find this natural sound. You can do this exercise standing or sitting.

Exercise 2k: "The Elevator"

i) Start by deliberately placing your voice in your head area. Use an "mmmmm" sound, and then imagine that this sound is travelling down through your body as if it was in an elevator. Go down floor by floor, down through your face, neck and into your chest. When it has arrived in your chest open the hum into an "ah" sound. Then say, "Good morning, my name is…" Do not push your voice down into an artificially deep sound. As before, what you will find is that, as you relax and let the chest resonator come into play, your voice will naturally drop down a couple of notes, and also sound deeper because of the extra resonance.

VOCAL EXPRESSIVENESS

Now that you are finding your natural voice it is time to extend its range,

"The Elevator"

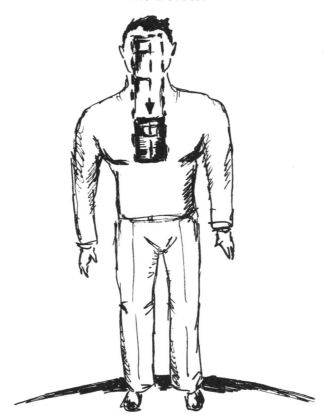

and understand more about language. There is a big difference between consonants and vowels. The former carry structure and meaning, the latter carry feeling. With consonants you stop the sound in a percussive way, with vowels you can lean languidly into them.

An important part of voice work is rediscovering the pure enjoyment of making sound and forming it into the richness of language. We all too easily forget this pleasure, as our speaking becomes functional, and our culture more and more visual. The following exercises are deliberately playful. Management guru Arie de Geus remarked: "To play is to learn. The essence of learning is discovery through play." Nothing could be truer of voice work. If you have any difficulty with the idea of playing – as many logically focused adults do – make a note. It may be useful data for the "Inner Critic" chapter…

Let's take a look at how we can extend our vocal range.

Exercise 2l: Consonants and Vowels

i) Work your way through the consonants, taking time to explore each one – bbbbbbb, ccccccc, ddddddd etc. Speak them slowly, now quickly. Speak in a high pitch, now a low pitch, now in between. Notice how each one involves a different shape in your mouth, and different use of your tongue. Notice the sharp percussive energy you can use with consonants, slightly different with each one. Exaggerate. We get very lazy in how we speak. Use this exercise to rediscover how distinct each consonant is.

ii) Go through a similar process with each vowel. Speak and sing each one, high and low, and in between. Feel each one resonate in your body. Notice how very different this is from the consonants.

Exercise 2m: Tongue Twisters

Another fun way to loosen up the jaw and mouth is to use tongue twisters.

i) Try "The lips and the teeth and tip of the tongue", getting faster and faster. Also "Peter Piper picked a peck of pickled pepper" or "Red Lorry, Yellow Lorry".

Now let's graduate to pieces of text. You can use ours or find your own. These are short poems and excerpts. When you work with these, exaggerate your expressiveness. Let your voice capture the mood and feeling of the words as fully as you can. We will give you suggestions to try out. Remember, you are *rehearsing*; there is no failure, only learning opportunities.

Exercise 2n: Speaking Poetry

Poetry is a great place to start exploring vocal expression. Each poet has their own point of view. Each poem is its own little world. Have fun and enjoy playing with the words.

i) This first poem is rich in consonants. Give each one as much expression as you can. Try to capture the wonder and excitement of the author, and the relentlessly building rhythm of the last three lines. It's called *Spring Rhythm*, written by our colleague William Ayot:

> *Turned a corner, saw Magnolia, folded-over*
> *sugar-pinkness, bright against the brittle blue.*
> *Saw Quince, saw brick red blossom Quince,*
> *standing bashful by a wall. Saw Witch-hazel,*
> *saw Cyclamen, saw Daisy, beaming like kids*
> *with a secret.*
> *Heard Jay, heard Finch, heard*
> *Robin and Wren. Heard Blackbird chortling*
> *like a winner at the bookies. Heard Moorhen*
> *with her wittering chicks.*
> *Then I heard Swan*
> *beat the sky like a drum. And I followed her*
> *rhythm and came to the heart of it and seeing*
> *became hearing and hearing became feeling*
> *and I knew what I felt and at last I said, Yes!*

ii) Here is a poem that contains a very different feeling, a sensuous and intimate connection with the forest. Try speaking it quietly, as though you were sharing an important personal secret with someone. Let your voice settle into its most relaxed and open sound. The poem is called *Sleeping in the Forest*, written by the American poet Mary Oliver:

> *I thought the earth*
> *remembered me, she*
> *took me back so tenderly, arranging*
> *her dark skirts, her pockets*
> *full of lichens and seeds. I slept*
> *as never before, a stone*
> *on the riverbed, nothing*
> *between me and the white fire of the stars*
> *but my thoughts, and they floated*

light as moths among the branches
of the perfect trees. All night
I heard the small kingdoms breathing
around me, the insects, and the birds
who do their work in the darkness.
All night I rose and fell, as if in water,
grappling with a luminous doom. By morning
I had vanished at least a dozen times
into something better.

iii) Finally, here is a wonderfully playful little poem. See if you can capture the childlike exuberance of the first seven lines, building in volume, and then create a mood change in the last line. It's called *The Leader*, written by the poet Roger McGough:

I wanna be the leader
I wanna be the leader
Can I be the leader?
Can I? I can?
Promise? Promise?
Yippee, I'm the leader
I'm the leader!

OK what shall we do?

VOLUME

Some people use too little volume when they present, some people too much. Both are off-putting to an audience. One last step in our vocal work is for you to practise increasing the power of your voice by using more breath and energy, rather than by shouting.

Some clients make the mistake of going into a presentation and speaking with the same energy as they used in a one-to-one conversation in the corridor outside. The performance situation requires more energy at all levels, including your voice. How much more depends on the size of your audience and the size of the space.

"Vocal Energy – One-to-one conversation"

"Vocal Energy – A larger audience"

Exercise 2o: Practising Vocal Energy Levels

This exercise is best done with a colleague in a large space, though if no-one is available you can imagine someone you are speaking to. You will need a short piece of text to work with – anything will do.

i) Energy Level 1: stand quite close to each other and speak to your colleague in a normal, everyday voice.

ii) Energy Level 2: stand about 5 metres apart. Speak your text again, using more energy, until your colleague indicates that he/she can clearly hear you.

iii) Energy Level 3: stand as far apart as you can – at least 10 metres. If you are in an auditorium, have your colleague go and sit in the audience. Speak again with more energy until your colleague is satisfied with how your voice is carrying.

Note: At first you may find that you start to shout. If you do, notice that you probably push your head forward and up (thus restricting the vocal cords), and generally tense your body. Vocal power comes through grounding, relaxed alertness, focus and the mobilization of your energy through your body.

iv) To succeed at Level 3 you need to be grounded. Push your feet down into the ground. Keep your knees relaxed. Use more breath. Mobilize your energy, and the maximum support of your lower body, so you are relaxed but alert. Feel your hips/pelvis as being the centre of your body, and the centre of your energy. And learn to TRUST this sensation.

VOCAL WARM-UP AND FINAL THOUGHTS

The above exercises will expand your vocal range and strength. You can also use a condensed version as an effective "warm-up" to get your voice into as good a shape as possible. We encourage you to try this following 10-minute sequence once or twice in the days before your next presentation, then do it on the day itself, as close to your presentation time as possible. The more you have worked with the exercises above, the more effective the following sequence will be.

Exercise 2p: Vocal Warm-up

i) Massage your face. Loosen the jaw (1 minute).

ii) Align your body, head, shoulders and spine; get grounded and breathing deeply (2 minutes).

iii) Use sounds "zzzzzzz", "sssssss", "haw" and "hoo" . Breathe deeply, without lifting your shoulders (2 minutes).

iv) Use "The Elevator" exercise to find your natural note. Go from the "ah" sound into "Good morning, my name is..." and other simple sentences (2 minutes).

v) Speak some tongue twisters, getting as fast as you can while staying accurate (1 minute).

vi) Speak some sentences from your next presentation (2 minutes).

We have offered you a range of exercises to help you develop your voice. To get maximum benefit you will need to practise these regularly for an initial period of at least two weeks, then return to them as and when you need. We both find that, as with all the other skills in this book, the more we practise the luckier we get!

Vocal awareness adds depth to your presence and heightens your impact. It allows you to find the right voice for the right occasion, to own your natural voice and to vary the range of pitch and volume. Perhaps most importantly, a developed voice can carry the intellectual, imaginative and emotional meaning of what we wish to communicate to others. As a performer in presentations, your voice is one of the most important parts of your equipment. As you find your true voice, and its natural expressiveness, you will deliver your material in a more spirited, animated way. People will hear you, and enjoy hearing you.

PART 2

Overcoming the Blocks

Chapter 3

The Inner Critic

In Part 1 we introduced you to the foundations of Presence and Voice. Now it's time to look at what might be stopping us being Present and vocally expressive in public presentations – the blocks.

NERVES ARE NOT THE PROBLEM

Many of the people we coach arrive with a similar complaint; "I get nervous when I have to present." We will help you identify where the nervousness comes from and help you to put it to good use. Being nervous is not – in and of itself – a bad thing. It is natural to become nervous when we stand in front of a group of people. Throughout history, for most peoples, being the centre of attention is both an opportunity and a potential threat. This stimulates the production of adrenalin in the body and can, at best, give us a heightened sense of awareness. It also gives us access to more energy, which we will need to make an impact on a group.

Richard's father, Laurence Olivier, was a successful actor for over 50 years. A reporter once asked him, towards the end of his life, when he stopped getting nervous. He replied; "The day I stop getting nervous is the day *after* I should have stopped!" Being in front of a crowd is not a "normal" occurrence; it is "special" and requires a special energy. Remember; Presentation *is* Performance.

We use the image of "riding a tiger", with you being the rider and your nerves the tiger. If the nerves have you, it feels like you are being dragged off on a wild animal over whom you have no control, and whom you have good reason to fear. If you stop your nerves altogether it is like watching a tame, doped-up tiger in a circus (claws and teeth removed for safety). But there is no "bite" and no interest. However, if you and the tiger are "in flow" there is an exciting edge that others enjoy watching.

So it is not the nerves, in and of themselves, that cause the problem.

INTRODUCING THE INNER CRITIC

After working with actors and managers for over 15 years we think the answer is actually quite simple. It is the negative messages you give yourself about your performance that do the damage, by evoking a distracting anxiety. These messages are what we refer to as the "Inner Critic". For the rest of this chapter we will explore what these messages are and how they came about. In the next chapter we will help you work towards a helpful alternative, the "Inner Coach".

In our experience, the principal reason people under-perform in front of groups is the Inner Critic they hear speaking inside their own head. This is both the good news and the bad news. The good news is that because the problem is in your mind, the solution is too. The bad news is that the Inner Critic has probably been there a long time and may take some shifting.

We all have an internal dialogue going on most of the time – an inner voice that comments about what's going on and what we think about it. You might want to practise a little inner attention and see if you can catch your internal voice right now. What are you saying to yourself about this idea right now? Can you hear it? If not, don't worry – just keep checking your thought process every now and again. This practice will prepare you to identify the Inner Critic.

HOW THE INNER CRITIC DEVELOPED

The Inner Critic is the result of a natural evolutionary process that uses the lessons of the past to inform the present. We remember messages we received about a certain situation and internalize them as "learning" that "teaches" us how to respond when a similar situation triggers the memory. This ability is one of the human gifts. We use this gift in numerous different circumstances, often without being conscious of it, and it can be extremely helpful.

For example, when we stand on the pavement ready to cross a road many of us will hear an inner commandment that says "Look before you cross", or some near equivalent. Now, these words can usually be traced back to a voice that was at one time external to us – a parent or guardian from childhood. But over time it has become internalized, and we create the inner voice without an external stimulus. We hear the commandment and do what it says. That is to say that when we recognize a situation similar to one from the past (waiting to cross a road) we have a recorded message in our heads that repeats the original commandment ("Look before you cross"). This voice may well have saved our life at some point so we have reason to remember it. It is still useful.

However, there are some inner voices that have outlived their usefulness. To use a modern metaphor, it is like bits of an old computer system that have become hard wired, even though their original purpose has been served and they are not required any more.

> When Richard was growing up, lots of family friends would ask; "And what are you going to do when you grow up, become an actor like your dad?" An innocent enough question, "Except that over the years I found myself saying 'Oh no, I'm not the one in the family who does that.' Then, once I had established myself as a theatre director, I would occasionally be asked to give a public lecture. They were torture. Throughout the talk I couldn't stop hearing an inner voice saying 'You're not the one in your family who does this, you're in the wrong place!' Although the fact was no longer true, the voice was still in the system, ingrained, and hard to shake off.

In our early work with critical voices we were inspired by Augusto Boal, a renowned Brazilian theatre director and social activist. He had spent years developing theatrical exercises that allow oppressed peoples to express their reality in a safe theatrical forum. A few years ago he was asked to experiment with his methods in Paris for three months but remained dubious, as he believed "free" peoples in the West did not suffer oppression. However, after the three month experiment he exclaimed; "I see now that people in the West are just as oppressed as people from my country, the difference is, they do it to themselves." He coined a phrase to describe this, "Les flics dans la tête" ("The cops in the head"). It a good way of describing the critical voices, the internal policing system that keeps you from expressing yourself freely and confidently.

An old saying maintains that we spend the first year of our lives being told to "stand up and talk" and the rest of our childhood being told to "sit down and shut up!" The trouble is, many of us internalized this type of external voice from childhood. So now it has become a "cop in the head". When we stand up to deliver a presentation, we hear the "cop" as an internal voice commanding us to "sit down and shut up!"

"The Cop in the Head"

This Inner Critic is a mental stimulus that provokes a physical and/or emotional response. It is this automatic response to the inner critical voice that inhibits us from giving a confident performance. We will endeavour to unlock both the Critic and the response from your system.

FINDING THE INNER CRITIC

As with much of what we teach, the key to improvement starts with awareness. You need to notice the internal voices in your mind and pay particular attention to those that have a critical or judgemental tone about your actions. The ones that sound something like "There you go, I knew you would get that wrong, you always do."

> Karen works for a scientific journal. She has to present new physics findings to the general press. She arrived stating that she always felt uneasy during these briefings, but did not know why. During the course she was able to identify a critical voice that operated inside her head during these press briefings. It said "You're boring them – they don't have any idea what you are talking about." We asked her to speak this voice out loud in the tone in which she heard it. She spoke the words again – with a warning tone that would be guaranteed to unsettle a presenter. When we repeated the words back to her in the same tone, it suddenly became clear to her why she felt unease. It was a natural response that most of us would share when hearing these words during a presentation. This was her Inner Critic.

Over the years we have helped clients identify hundreds of these Inner Critics. Although many are unique and individual, others fall into a more typical range. The Critic manifests in both the "I" and "you" form. The most common voices seem to cluster around the following themes:

"You're going to get too nervous and muck it all up!"

"They don't want to listen to what I've got to say."

"I don't have anything worthwhile to say, I'm wasting their valuable time."

"They don't want to listen to you, you are not important."

"You're going to forget something important."

"I don't feel safe."

"You won't get it right."

"I haven't prepared properly – someone is going to challenge me and I won't be able to answer."

"Anything less than perfect is not good enough!"

These are some of the most popular critics. They all do a pretty good job of unsettling a presenter. So, if you feel nerves before or during a presentation in an unhelpful way, chances are that you have got an Inner Critic coming along for the ride. The following two exercises involve "Active Imagination". This means that you are guiding yourself through what you might think of as a day-dream, except it is not guiding you, you are in control – being active not passive in the imagining.

Exercise 3a: Identifying the Inner Critic

i) Active Imagination (this exercise will take 5–10 minutes). When you have the time and the space, get your journal ready; try and make sure you won't be disturbed. Sit down, close your eyes and imagine yourself walking into a room to give an important presentation. Picture the room and the people as clearly as you can. Now try and catch what thoughts, worries and concerns would be running through your head as you take your place in front of this group. What would you be assuming about this situation? Would you feel confident and OK in yourself or not? Would you feel comfortable or not? And if not, why not? What would be the messages you would typically give yourself in this situation? Try and catch what the Inner Critic might say to you. Trust your first thoughts and intuitions. Write them down in your journal.

ii) Practical Identification. If the Active Imagination exercise does not yield clear results for you, you can, of course, wait until your next public presentation. Practise developing Presence and maintaining Dual Attention – try and be aware of what is going on in you as well as what is going on in the room. Notice the thoughts, assumptions and voices operating inside you before and during your piece. What messages are you giving yourself about this situation? Note them down as soon as you get the chance.

If the practice of tracking inner thoughts is difficult for you, be patient. You may need to attempt the exercises a few times before the real Inner Critic becomes apparent. Remember, you are attempting to identify the inner thoughts and voices that have a negative effect on your performance. There may be a few of them operating, and different ones may operate in different situations, so don't worry if you get more than one. It is all useful homework and essential preparation before you will be ready to manage the Inner Critic effectively.

EFFECTS AND NET RESULTS

The first step is to become aware of the Inner Critic and identify what they say to you. The next step is to recognize the physical and emotional impact this has on you.

> Sheila was a middle manager in a large food company. A recent promotion entailed regular presentations to groups of buyers. However, she always felt rushed and always spoke too quickly. We asked her to track the messages she gave herself during her next presentation. She reported one voice that said "These are pretty important people – they don't have much time", and another which said, "You are going to get nervous and rush." We set up a simple role-play exercise, where she would begin a presentation and other participants would externalize her inner voices and speak them out loud to her as she began speaking. We then stopped the role-play and asked her to notice what effect – physical and emotional –the voices were having on her. She immediately reported that the palms of her hands had become sweaty, she felt her cheeks blush and felt embarrassed. The result was that she wanted to finish as quickly as she could and get off the platform, fast. It ended up creating a self-fulfilling prophecy; the Inner Critic in her mind provoked a response that created the very result she was worried about. She immediately recognized this pattern as a major cause of her current problem with presenting.

Each one of us is likely to manifest our own unique combination of effects and net results; we have collected examples of the most popular. Notice which ones feel most familiar to you.

Physical effects – presenters often report sweaty palms, "butterflies" in the stomach, nausea, headache, shaking legs, clenching fists, excessive and/or rapid movements (hands, hopping about, pacing back and forth), and looking at the floor.

Emotional effects – presenters often feel embarrassed, shy, foolish, insecure, dejected, guarded, suspicious, resigned, overwhelmed, hopeless, incapable, humiliated, harassed, resentful, irritated, hostile, apathetic, empty, lost or numb.

Net results – presenters often end up: losing focus, speeding up, forgetting what to say next, not making eye contact with the audience, only hearing the Inner Critic, wanting to leave the room, wanting a hole to open up and swallow them, becoming convinced that the audience is the enemy, trying to get it over as soon as possible.

These are a small but fairly typical selection of effects and net results. So what happens to you?

Exercise 3b: Identifying the Effects and Net Results of the Inner Critic

i) Active Imagination (this exercise requires 5–10 minutes undisturbed). Select one or two of the critical voices you have identified as having a negative impact on your presentations. Imagine yourself back in presentation mode and hear the Inner Critic speak. (You can do this in your mind or speak out loud.) Now check the effects. Physical – what happens in your body when you hear the Inner Critic? Emotional – what do you feel? Now see if you can remember or imagine what the net result of these effects is on your performance. Write any information down in your journal.
ii) Practical Identification. Even if the Active Imagination exercise has given you useful information, identifying the effects of the Inner Critic is worth checking out in practice. During an upcoming presentation or meeting where you have to speak, track your internal state before, during and after your turn. Was the Active Imagination accurate? Were there other effects and results, other than those you imagined there would be? Again, write them down as soon as you can.

The more we become aware of what is actually happening during a presentation, the more likely we will be able to remedy it. So, if you have now identified the content of the Inner Critic, and explored its effects and net results, it is time to go a little deeper...

TRACKING THE ORIGIN

All Inner Critics exist for a reason. At some time in our past we received a message or internalized some learning that enabled them to embed themselves in our consciousness. So the next step is to try and identify why they came to be there in the first place.

If you read the following and cannot track the origin clearly, you can still take effective steps to counteract the negative influence. But if you can identify the likely original roots of the problem, the solution may become that much clearer.

There are two main causes of an Inner Critic. The first is when we internalize an external voice (like "Look before you cross"). This was a phrase originally said by someone else, usually someone who had some kind of authority over us, or whose opinion we respected (or both). We believed what they said and internalized the words as a belief about how things are (in relation to this kind of situation). When a new situation reminds us of the original situation in which we heard the external voice speak, our mind produces the internalized critical voice.

The second cause is similar, except that instead of an external voice which you simply internalized, this route is caused by an external event about which you made an assumption. No outer voice was involved but internalized learning happened anyway.

> Richard's Inner Critic that said "You're not the one in the family who acts" was learning internalized from an event at school:
>
> "When I was nine I was cast in a leading role in a school play. I had no idea what it really entailed and for some reason a group of friends and I never got down to learning our lines. When it became clear that none of us would be off script by performance time, the play was cancelled. No-one actually tried to blame me but I took it as a tremendous failure. I remember thinking 'Maybe this acting thing is not for me.' Even as the conscious memory of the actual event faded over the next few years, by the time I was in my teens I was convinced that 'I am not the one in the family who does that'.

So while the cause can be either an external voice or an event, the effect ends up the same. The sequence usually follows this pattern:

1 Someone said something
Or something happened

2 You believed what someone said
Or you made an assumption about the event

3 You internalized the belief *Or* assumption

4 It began operating in your head as a critical voice

5 Now it affects your performance when you present in public.

The effect is a result of what you are telling yourself, and that is due to a belief or assumption from the past, but which is still in your system in the present. (This same system operates in a similar way in many areas of life and work. While our focus in this book is Peak Performance Presentations, you can apply the learning in different areas as you wish.)

Internalizing an External Voice

Sarah is an extremely capable finance officer working for a large media corporation. She came from a very academic background where success was measured in university degrees and PhD's. Although it was not assessed at the time, she since discovered that she has mild dyslexia and often reads words the wrong way round. For a period during her childhood her mother took time off work to help her with her reading. Often getting frustrated with her daughter's inability to do what she was taught she was often told "Now you're being stupid, how on earth are you going to make anything of yourself if you go on behaving like that?" Perhaps a typical expression from a hard-working, frustrated parent, but that voice was now paralysing Sarah in her working life. Every time she tried to make a presentation to the Senior Management Team the Inner Critic would kick off – "Now you're being stupid..." – which would, of course, shut down her ability to express herself powerfully to the group in question.

Internalizing an Assumption based on External Events

Brian, a manager in a large telecommunications company, had recently been appointed to a position where, for the first time, he had to report directly to the board to get his budget approved. He had been referred for coaching because he was coming across as extremely defensive, and at times aggressive, in his board presentations, saying the equivalent of "You will approve this budget because it is the only sensible thing to do…" – which wasn't going down well at all. A day into the course he became aware of the Inner Critic, which said "Don't let them humiliate you!" This made him stiffen up and push harder for what he wanted. He now saw that this was the root cause of the problem. We then coached him to think back through his many experiences to try and determine the original experience that had created the voice. It didn't take him long. He soon remembered being brought up in a small country village and attending the local school run by a sadistic headmaster. This headmaster would spend the weekly assembly calling out some unfortunate youth to stand next to him, and would then proceed to humiliate them in front of the whole school. Brian spent a large part of his schooldays determined not to do anything that would make him stand out enough to be called out front by this headmaster – "Don't let him humiliate you" had become his unconscious motto.

Now, 30 years later, the voice was still operating. The recent promotion had brought him face to face with those he perceived to be in a similar position of authority as the headmaster – the board. And he was reacting to being in their presence in the same way he had learned to act in front of the headmaster – "Defend yourself, stick to your ground and don't let them humiliate you."

It is important to remember that the Inner Critic often starts as a necessary survival strategy. It was wise for Brian to be alert at school, his careful actions helped him avoid the abusive attention of the headmaster. But the Critic was now applying this teaching to *all* authority figures. Rather than helping Brian survive, it was now putting his career at risk. It had outlived its usefulness but was still "plugged in" to Brian's system. Once he had identified the origin of his Critic, he was one step closer to unplugging it.

So, are you ready to investigate the origins of your Inner Critic?

The next exercise may take only a few minutes – you may have been reflecting on possible origins as you read about our examples – or it may take a while. For some people the origins may be diffuse, maybe because it was a very early memory or maybe because the Critic was slowly built up over a period of time, with no clear and obvious external voices or events currently available to your mind.

Some people even find that they are in the grip of a "cultural" Inner Critic, which does not necessarily manifest as a personal memory but as part of a cultural identity. While these are often dismissed as stereotypes, our experience is that some of them actually contain more than a bit of truth, whether it be the unemotional "stiff upper lip" public school Englishman, the unassertive Asian woman, the unfunny German, the over-talkative Italian etc. While they are by no means true for all, or even most, people in a culture, they are true for some, or the stereotype would not have emerged in the first place. So, if no personal memories arise, think back to your parents and their ancestry; what hidden messages might you be carrying from them?

Don't worry if it takes some time – sit with the notion for a while and some possibilities will usually float to the surface. When you're ready, have a go.

Exercise 3c: Tracking the Origin of the Inner Critic

Pick an Inner Critic you identified in Exercise 3a) and reflect on its potential origin. Where might this voice have originated? It might be anywhere from pre-verbal childhood to the recent past. You are looking for some experience – or a cluster of experiences – which could have convinced you that this assumption or belief was correct. At the time it was a realistic external voice you heard or a reasonable internal assumption you made about a situation or event. How might the voice have been formed? Write down any thoughts, memories or intuitions that seem remotely relevant.

As you move through the rest of this book, and practise the suggested exercises, you might become aware of other voices that emerge, especially as you try to expand your repertoire and practise authenticity. Whatever they are, notice them and write them down. You may choose to work with them later.

In the meantime we would like to leave this chapter with the words of a brave poet, Mary Oliver, who survived a long struggle with her inner voices as they tried to hold her back from fulfilling her potential. In the end she won, and this poem is living proof, but the journey wasn't easy...

THE JOURNEY

One day you finally knew
what you had to do, and began,
though the voices around you
kept shouting
their bad advice –
though the whole house
began to tremble
and you felt the old tug
at your ankles.
"Mend my life!"
each voice cried.
But you didn't stop.
You knew what you had to do,
though the wind pried
with its stiff fingers
at the very foundations,
though their melancholy
was terrible.
It was already late
enough, and a wild night,
and the road full of fallen
branches and stones.
But little by little,
as you left their voices behind,
the stars behind to burn
through the sheets of clouds,
and there was a new voice
which you slowly
recognized as your own,

that kept you company
as you strode deeper and deeper
into the world,
determined to do
the only thing you could do –
determined to save
the only life you could save.

Chapter 4

The Inner Coach

In this chapter we will help you build up internal resources to counteract the negative effect of nerves and the Inner Critics that get in your way. We will introduce you to the concept of "Sense Memory" and explain how you can develop your own "Inner Coach". Instead of that critical voice sounding in your head when you get up to present, how would it be to imagine a friendly coach, giving helpful advice and encouraging you to do your best?

It may sound over-optimistic to you right now, but more importantly… *it works*! With some imaginative work and regular practice you can develop just the right positive inner images and voices to act as an antidote to the negative voices and effects you have previously identified. These new inner resources will end up being as helpful to you in the future as the old system has proved to be unhelpful in the past.

As became clear in the last chapter, our past memories and experiences have an impact on the present. Some of these memories, as you hopefully discovered for yourself, have contributed to the development of the Inner Critic. The good news is that we can use other memories – with a more positive flavour – to make us feel more at ease. We can, if we wish, even create new "memories" that will help us develop the Inner Coach and sustain a positive effect in future presentations.

SENSE MEMORY

All peak performers, whether actors, sports professionals or politicians, have developed their own inner resources to enable them to be at their best in the spotlight. They know that you can't just walk from the parking lot to the stage, field or conference room and hope to be ready to meet the expectations of the audience.

We will give you a complete guide to preparing yourself for Peak Performance in the final chapter. Here we focus on some of the key techniques you can use to get yourself in the right frame of mind before and during a presentation.

The great Russian acting teacher Constantin Stanislavsky developed an exercise he called "Sense Memory". He noticed that many actors were simulating or faking the emotion that their character was required to portray in front of an audience. He saw that this came across as inauthentic and lacked genuine impact. So he started asking his actors, during rehearsal, to sit down and recall a time in their lives when they had come closest to experiencing the emotional state that their character was going through in a particular scene. He asked them to really "sense" the memory, imagine it was happening in the present, right now, and got them to notice the effect it was having on their state – physical, emotional and mental. Then he would ask them to start the relevant scene, holding this "sensed memory" in mind. The actors would always reach a more genuine state, and achieve greater impact.

This technique was imported to the West after the Second World War and many great actors of the last two generations have used it, including Marlon Brando, Robert de Niro and Al Pacino. While they would use it to achieve a whole range of emotional states, we can use a simple version to help us.

When Richard was asked to do a book tour in America in 1995 he accepted with some trepidation:

"I was used to presenting other authors' ideas to people; suddenly sharing my own was more than a little frightening. I asked Nicholas to help me use some of our favourite rehearsal techniques to prepare me for this new level of performance. We chose the 'Sense Memory' exercise. We imagined that if we focused on remembering the things in life that make us feel good and confident, and brought these to mind just before speaking in public, it should have the same beneficial effect on us as the technique did on actors preparing to perform.

We came up with a simple list of when we tended to feel at our best; being in our favourite places, doing our favourite things and being with our favourite people. As an afterthought we added remembering those times when people we respected gave us unsolicited positive feedback.

So, as part of my presentation homework I made a list related to all of these and noted how each one made me feel. Then I chose one item from each list that I intuited as particularly compelling. Out of my first list I ended up choosing the following:

Place: lying on a beach in Spain listening to the waves breaking gently on the shore
Feeling: relaxed, peaceful
Activity: playing football with my children, Troy and Ali
Feeling: energized, joyful in sharing knowledge and experience
Person: my wife, Shelley
Feeling: loving, connected
Statement: from a participant in a workshop; "You speak very powerfully"
Feeling: acknowledged, respected

When I made my selection, I sat down, closed my eyes and brought all four to mind, in sequence. After a couple of minutes I was feeling good, confident and ready for a public challenge. When I arrived for my first book tour date I made sure that I arrived at the lecture room early. I sat down, closed my eyes and recalled the positive memories I had chosen. Again the positive feelings flowed; I relaxed and started the lecture in a much better state than I could have hoped."

The following exercise will help you develop some inner resources of your own.

Exercise 4a: Sense Memory

This exercise will take about 10–20 minutes, undisturbed, with your journal close to hand. We recommend that you take this exercise step by step. Read each numbered section a couple of times, or until you are clear about the instructions, and then, when you feel ready, put the book down and begin.
i) Close your eyes and bring to mind your two or three favourite places in the world. With each one, take the time to really sense your memory. Imagine being there – "see" the environment, feel the temperature, remember why you love this place. Be aware of your physical, emotional

and mental state when you are in this place. Notice how it may change your current state of mind.

When you feel you have got a real sense of what each place gives you, slowly transfer your attention to the next one and repeat the process. When you are finished, open your eyes and make notes. What is the place and what is the feeling that comes with it?

ii) Repeat the steps from i) but with two or three of your favourite activities or hobbies. What is the activity and what is the feeling it gives you?

iii) Now do the same with two or three of your favourite people. Who are they and how do they make you feel when you are with them?

iv) Now do the same with your favourite positive role models – coaches, mentors, friends or strangers who have given you valued positive feedback. Remember what they said to you and how it made you feel. You might want to focus on the words you would particularly like to hear before an important presentation. Make a note of who it was and what they said.

v) Now look back through your notes. Choose one example from each category that you intuitively feel could have the best impact on your state before a presentation: one place, activity, person and statement.

Exercise 4b: Using Sense Memory before a Presentation

i) Next time you make a presentation, make sure you give yourself some preparation time before you start. Sit down quietly for a few minutes, practise the breathing you learnt in "Presence", and bring these positive memories into your mind. Let them soak into you, physically, emotionally and mentally, and allow them to add positive energy and feeling to your state of being.

ii) Write a brief report about the effect of using these inner resources.

Actors report that most "sense memories" have a natural life span. In other words, whatever past experience they use to create a present emotional state will work for a while, but eventually lose its potency. The same may be true for you. The memories you choose first should work – for a while – but eventually you might find that the "magic" wears off. At which point simply choose another set of images and memories to

"Sense Memory"

bring to mind. If you use up the magic in everything you have noted so far, then make another list!

Sense Memory will help you get into a positive state of mind before important meetings and presentations. But if you have a persistent Inner Critic, you may need to develop a more effective antidote – the Inner Coach.

INTRODUCING THE INNER COACH

In our development of the Inner Coach we have worked closely with Dutch Psychiatrist Dr Lowijs Perquin and the Pesso Boyden Psychomotor System. Albert Pesso and Diane Boyden were working with dancers in the late 1960s when they realized that some dancers were unable to perform certain movements. On more investigation they discovered that these dancers had built up muscle patterns due to an inner voice based on early life experiences – much like our Inner Critic. The physical rigidity of these muscle patterns literally restricted the expressiveness of their movement. After further exploration they found that these muscles could be trained out of their habitual patterns, if the people concerned received the appropriate antidote. This was a new, positive voice capable of counteracting the negative effect of the old negative voice. When the new voice was heard from someone who was role-playing what they called an "ideal mother", "ideal father" or other ideal primary care-giver, it seemed to have that much more impact. They subsequently developed a powerful therapeutic system based on these initial discoveries. We will be drawing on this system and its effective approach as we invite you to develop your Inner Coach. (For more details see Further Resources.)

The good news is that the development of an Inner Coach follows the same basic steps as the development of an Inner Critic:

1 Someone says something

2 You believe it

3 You internalize the belief

4 It begins operating in your head as a positive voice

5 It affects your performance when you present in public.

This is the route to creating what we call a "new map". Hopefully, you have identified some inner critical voices that have a negative effect on your performance. This is the "old map". What we will work towards now is the new.

LEVEL 1 OR LEVEL 2?

As we move through the rest of this chapter there will be a time when you will have a choice as to what level of work you wish to engage with. Level 1 works to counteract the effect that the critical voices have on you in the present. Level 2 goes a step deeper to counteract the past causes of those same critical voices. The following examples should give you a sense of the difference and allow you to make the choice that feels right.

Level 1 Example

Steven arrived at a course as a bundle of energy and nerves. In his opening presentation he couldn't keep still for a second. He was walking about, rocking back and forth, shifting weight from one leg to the other and not really making eye contact with anyone. He said he had come because he wanted to feel more confident and less nervous in presentations. As the work progressed he became aware of a driving critical voice that believed that no-one was really interested in what he had to say. As a result he thought he had to put out a lot of energy to keep people from falling asleep and had to finish as quickly as possible. This belief was, of course, becoming a self-fulfilling prophecy. The more frenetic energy he put out, the less people would engage with what he was saying.

When it came to his turn for a coaching session we asked another group member to role-play the Inner Critic and speak that voice for him. We explained that we wanted to externalize the inner critical voice, in order that he could see and understand the effect it was having on him. We asked him to place the Critic somewhere in the room – he chose a spot directly across the room. As he started his presentation the role-player stood where Steven had indicated and, after a few seconds, said, in a critical voice, "They're not interested in what you are saying." Almost as soon as the Critic spoke, Steven started ramping up his energy level and making faster gestures. The Critic came in again, "They're still not listening" and Steven started speaking more quickly...

We stopped him and asked him if this was what was usually going on inside his head when he gave presentations. He ruefully admitted that it was remarkably similar. We pointed out the negative effect it was having on his performance, and suggested that what was missing from the situation was a Coach. Although we wanted him to develop an Inner Coach by the end of the course, it would be useful to start with an External Coach. He picked one of the other group members to role-play a Coach. We asked

Steven to place the Coach somewhere in the room and to give him the words he would really want to hear from such a figure. He thought for a while and then asked the Coach to stand behind his right shoulder. He wanted to hear the Coach say; "What you have to say is important. You are doing fine and they are listening."

So on Take Two we asked Steven to pause each time the Critic spoke and listen to the Coach as well, before he continued. He started again; the Critic spoke, Steven paused, the Coach spoke and Steven continued. This happened a couple of times, but the difference in Steven was immediately apparent. No longer subjected to a lone critical voice, he did not feel the need to push his energy up and rush on. He paused, waited for the Coach to provide the antidote to the Critic, gathered himself and continued in a calmer manner and at a slower pace.

When Steven finished, he smiled broadly and his audience applauded. He had not only survived the criticism but had genuinely engaged his audience as well. The difference was clear and effective.

Level 2 Example

Paul was a high-flying young executive, already in a senior management role in a large sports organization. Outwardly very confident, Paul recognized a major flaw in his presentation delivery. He was always on the lookout for someone who appeared not to like what he was saying. As soon as he noticed anyone in his audience who looked blank or perhaps slightly hostile, he became obsessed with making this person like him. This would dominate his awareness for the rest of the presentation and distract him from his real task.

We asked him to choose a fellow participant who could role-play a "Hostile Audience Member". He did so and placed this man on the left-hand side of the audience he was addressing. Paul started, but as soon as he looked in the direction of the role-player he became noticeably anxious. He reported hearing the Inner Critic telling him "You're not good enough, he doesn't like you. This is going to be trouble!" Immediately he felt an uncomfortable tightening in his stomach and an overall sense of unease.

When asked whether he could remember any experiences that could have initially provoked this kind of reaction he talked of a period in his life between the ages of 10 and 14. Brought up in a religious family he would give readings every Sunday in a local church. After every reading a senior community member would give him critical feedback, in front of everyone. He felt terrible and began to dread the next reading. Each time he would look out for this "Community Critic" and try to get him on his side. Each time he would fail and receive a variation of the message "It's not really good enough, is it? A week to practise and still lots of mistakes!"

We gave Paul a choice of which level he wanted to work at and he opted for Level 2. Now we asked him to pick someone to play the Ideal Coach. This would be a figure who, had he (or she) been there back then, would have given Paul a very different, positive message. Another group member was duly picked and agreed to play the role of a "Friendly Community Member". Paul was invited to think about what words he would most have wanted to hear in the original situation. He came up with; "You did really well... this is very difficult for an 11-year old and you are making such good progress."

We were going to role-play the scene from the past but with an added ingredient from the present – Paul's awareness of what he needed to hear back then. This new positive experience would be the beginning of a new map and could help antidote the original negative message.

Paul set the scene, imagining himself to be aged 11, and had the Coach stand just behind his right shoulder. As Paul finished his reading the Coach spoke; "You did really well... this is very difficult for an 11-year old and you are making such good progress."

Paul smiled shyly, as if he could not quite believe this new voice. We asked him if he was really able to imagine he was receiving this message as an 11-year old boy. He tried again and smiled more broadly, less shyly. The scene was repeated three more times, each time the positive message seemed to sink in more deeply. By the end Paul was beaming, his face more open and relaxed than we had seen it so far in the programme.

When he felt ready we asked him to imagine himself moving forward in time, but with the experience of the Ideal Coach still with him. Now, back in the present scene we had started with, he was able to look at the "Hostile

Audience Member" without being phased or feeling uneasy. He was able to face him squarely and confidently. He felt free of the old pull to make this person like him.

The key difference between the Level 1 and 2 options is in the time-frame of the antidote. Level 1 works to counter the Inner Critic as it manifests in your present working experience, while Level 2 works with an Inner Coach who "travels back through time" to antidote an original cause of the Inner Critic.

You may decide to choose Level 1 because it feels right, or you think it will serve you just as well as Level 2, or even because you don't currently have access to the relevant historical scenes/old memories that you need for Level 2. Even if you know that you want to work at Level 2, it is important to read the following sections as part of your preparation.

CREATING AN ANTIDOTE – LEVEL 1

This work is designed to help you release yourself from the inhibitions imposed by the old map. In our programmes we create a rehearsal environment where clients can get a bodily experience of the antidote to hold up against the Inner Critic. Experience shows that even by ourselves we can create a powerful antidote in our mind, which we can then practise in actuality. By imagining the desired future and then "acting it into the body" we create a new potential which, with further rehearsal and commitment, can become a new reality.

Although we will start with a mental exercise, the key to success is a "felt experience" – which is a combination of the body and mind. The mind starts the process, the emotions and the body feel it. The combination is powerful and memorable.

We will work towards this goal in manageable steps. Before we experience the Inner Coach in full, we need to figure out what we want them to say. The right words will become the antidote that diminishes the power of the Inner Critic. The antidote is the perfect remedy to counteract the "poison" created by the critical voices.

"Old Map"

Exercise 4c: Creating an Antidote – Level 1

This exercise will take you 10–20 minutes, undisturbed, with journal and pen at hand. A couple of important pointers. First, you should always link the antidote as directly as you can to the original voice. For example,

"New Map"

"You're going to bore them" could be antidoted by a coaching voice that says "You are interesting and they will be interested in what you say." Secondly, always create a positive antidote. For example, "You are interesting" is positive, whereas "You are not boring" is a double negative. **i)** Read through your journal and reflect on the inner critical voices you have noted so far. Mark the ones that you sense have the biggest impact on you. When you have finished, pick one. Which do you instinctively feel is "the big one"? You can always repeat the exercise with others later.

ii) Now look at it and come up with a few potential antidotes. What would the opposite of this message be? What is it that you would most like to hear in place of this voice? Jot down versions and variations as you wish. When you have finished select the one you feel will be the most helpful.

Now you have a sense of what you want to hear, it is time to investigate whom you want to hear it from.

FINDING THE INNER COACH – LEVEL 1

You may have found some powerful old memories during the Sense Memory exercise to help you prepare yourself before presentations. Here we will embark on a process that will create some effective "new memories" that will serve to further antidote the negative effect of the Inner Critic. We will seek to add a new Active Imagination or "new memory" to your actual old memories, good and bad. This is the time for you to focus your imaginative powers on the creation of an Inner Coach. It is your experience of the Inner Coach that lies at the foundation of an effective "new map".

Exercise 4d: Imagining an Inner Coach – Level 1

This exercise will take you 10–20 minutes, undisturbed, with your journal and pen at hand.

Note: Although you may if you wish imagine a real person in your life as your Inner Coach, if you need to antidote a strong Inner Critic we advise you to imagine an "ideal" Inner Coach, who does not exist in reality. Unless the real person is actually going to be a true coach for you, the difference between your imagining and the actual reality will create a discrepancy that may undermine the power of the exercise. Read each section until you are clear about your task, then begin.

i) Relax. Practise a little gentle, deep breathing. Allow the words you created as an antidote to come into your mind. What tone of voice do you hear these words in? Who is it that you could imagine saying them? Allow an image of this Inner Coach to form in your mind. Look at their face, examine their features. Hear them saying the antidote message again. Allow yourself to take it in and believe it. Be aware of how this image makes you feel.

ii) Make some notes about the figure you imagined. How did they appear? How did they sound? How did you feel?

Now you have the right words and the right figure available, it is time to put them to work.

USING THE INNER COACH – LEVEL 1

Exercises 4c) and d) are the building blocks for the next exercise so please make sure you have completed them before moving on to 4e).

Exercise 4e: Active Imagination to Summon the Inner Coach – Level 1

The following exercise will take about 15–20 minutes, undisturbed, with your journal and pen at hand. It is an Active Imagination exercise. This means that you are guiding yourself through what you might think of as a day-dream, except it is not guiding you, *you* are in control. You are author and director, summoning appropriate images to form inside your head, in your mind's eye. Some people find this more difficult than others. Be patient and don't rush it. It may take a few tries to get all the way through to a positive result. Read the instructions a few times until you are clear about what you will be doing, then start when you are ready. (You may wish to have some cushions or blankets handy for props for section ii.)

i) Find a place to sit or stand, imagining you are about to start an important presentation. Close your eyes. Imagine the room you would be in and the people you would be speaking to. Let the voice of the Inner Critic speak inside your head. Register the effect it has on you. Now consciously summon the Inner Coach. Take the time to really imagine them being present in the room. Place them where you would most want them to be, wherever most suits you. See their face, feel their presence. Now let them speak. Hear them say the words you most want to hear before and during an important presentation. Let it sink in – and register the different impact this voice has on you. Try it again. Notice how you feel differently from when you only had the Inner Critic present.

ii) Begin to make a "body memory" of the feeling. Imagine you are able to take a photographic record of how you feel with the Inner Coach present. If you feel the support somewhere specific in your body (eg chest, stomach, back of the neck) gently place a hand there to reinforce the feeling with a physical sensation. If you want support in a place you cannot comfortably reach, move about or use props (leaning against a wall with a folded blanket behind you, sitting on or hugging a cushion etc) to reinforce the feeling. When it feels right, allow the Inner Coach to speak again. Really take in the message, as deeply as you can. Let it sink deep into the core of your being, reinforced by the physical sensation you have created to support the message. Allow yourself to believe what the Inner Coach is saying. Trust that they know you, they support you and they wish you well.

iii) Now, secure in your knowledge of the support from the Inner Coach, imagine the Inner Critic as a figure in the presentation room. As the Inner Coach reaffirms their positive message see the Inner Critic diminishing in importance and size. You may wish to imagine them disappearing or leaving the room altogether, at least being rendered impotent and ineffective in some way. Imagine taking a picture of this new scene, with the Inner Coach present giving support and the Inner Critic defeated, and store it in your memory bank. Know that you will be able to draw on this new picture whenever you need to. Take your time with this. Then, when you are ready, let the picture go and relax.

iv) We recommend that you write about your experience in your journal to further reinforce this "new memory".

When we imagine something powerfully we create a new groove in our memory bank. Many of us are able to recall striking images and stories from dreams as clearly as if they had actually happened. The same principle applies here. The image is "real" in your mind, and it is yours – your pictures, your antidote, your Inner Coach. Now you have this new figure in your image memory bank you can call on it whenever you wish to bring its positive message. As you rehearse summoning the Inner Coach you begin to reinforce the "new memory". Eventually, it will become as integrated a part of your system as the Inner Critic may have been up to now.

Exercise 4f: Summoning the Inner Coach for a Presentation – Level 1

i) Next time you know you will be entering a situation likely to trigger the Inner Critic, prepare yourself. If you can, go into the relevant room some time before the meeting/presentation is due to begin. Find the spot you will be sitting in and/or speaking from. Settle, breathe and ground yourself. Now imagine the Inner Coach being with you, in the appropriate place and speaking their words to you. Try and re-connect to the feeling you had in your Active Imagination rehearsal. Now imagine that your audience is in the room and the Inner Coach is still there, still supporting you. Let the Inner Coach speak to you again. Feel the added re-assurance this gives. Repeat as much of this as you can when the meeting/presentation actually starts. Especially if the Inner Critic shows up, simply take a deep breath and let the Inner Coach antidote their words. Remember the image of the defeated Inner Critic. The Inner Coach can and will help you

OR

ii) If you cannot actually get to "rehearse" in the room beforehand, simply find your own time and place to rehearse in your head. Bring the image of the Inner Coach into your mind's eye. This could be in your office, in the washroom or even through simply practising inner attention – and withdrawing some of your energy inside at any time. If you don't have any other options, you can even imagine your rehearsal while sitting in the room waiting for your time to speak.

iii) If there is a trusted colleague in the audience ask them afterwards for feedback. Did you come across more confidently etc?

iv) Make notes in your journal. What difference did the Inner Coach make? Did the antidote work? If so, keep going with this Inner Coach and their words. If not, repeat whatever steps are necessary until you create the ideal Inner Coach for you.

Remember, the more consciously you call on the Inner Coach, and the more often you do it, the more solid the new map becomes. While it will never eradicate the old map completely, it will give you a choice. Instead of your body being compelled to respond according to the old map, it now has a choice, because there is a new map in the system as well. The more you practise the luckier you get!

CREATING AN ANTIDOTE – LEVEL 2

Level 2 involves a little imaginative time travel – we will ask you to imagine what you needed at some point in the past but didn't get, and then imagine getting it, back then, at the very time you needed it. This different kind of "synthetic memory" seeks to repair the original damage, in your imagination. The imagined new scenes are the basis of the "new map", just as they are for Level 1. Whereas the Level 1 antidote is what you need to hear now, the Level 2 antidote is what you needed to hear "back then", but – for one reason or another – didn't.

Level 2 tends to be more powerful and lasting than Level 1. It is aimed at the root causes of the old map. The exercises have similar steps to Level 1, with the added complexity of managing the memories of the relevant past. This can, at times, stir up some uncomfortable feelings related to the original experience. While it is almost always possible to manage and contain these within the context of the exercise, if you are feeling particularly tired, stressed or vulnerable we would advise you not to engage in the following exercise until your state has changed for the better. If and when you feel ready, welcome to Level 2!

Exercise 4g: Creating an Antidote – Level 2

This exercise will take 10–20 minutes, undisturbed, with your journal and pen at hand. Remember to link the antidote directly to the original voice. For example, "Sit down and shut up!" could be antidoted by a coaching voice that says "I support you in standing up for yourself and speaking what you want to say." Find the positive expression of the antidote rather than the double negative; "I won't tell you to sit down and shut up."

i) Read through your journal and reflect on the origins of the inner critical voices you have noted so far. Let each memory reverberate briefly in your head and body. Make a mark by the ones that seem to have the most powerful impact on you – an inner emotional reaction is a sign that you are on the right track. When you have finished, pick one. Which do you instinctively feel is "the big one"? You can always repeat the exercise with others later.

ii) Now look at this memory/assumption and come up with a few potential antidotes. What is it that you would most like to hear in place of this old memory or assumption? Jot down as many versions and variations as you wish. When you have finished select the one you feel will be the most helpful.

Now you have a sense of what you want to hear, from whom do you want to hear it?

FINDING THE INNER COACH – LEVEL 2

The Inner Coach at Level 2 is a more complex figure and may take on a number of different guises. It is important that you find the right one for you. Just as the words should be the perfect antidote for what you originally heard or assumed, so the coaching figure should be the perfect antidote for the person you originally heard the negative message from.

If you are working with an inner belief created from an assumption you made about events (ie without a clear external voice attached) it is likely that this was due to the *absence* of a positive figure, rather than the presence of a negative figure. Your Inner Coach could therefore be a representative of an ideal figure who "would have been with you back then", even though your actual experience was of not getting support. Just as positive words can be the antidote to negative words, so someone who would have been present can antidote an actual experience of someone being absent. Your task, in this case, is to figure out who you would most have wanted to be present. Remember, you are creating an ideal figure.

We encourage you *not* to re-invent new personalities for actual people, because the discrepancy will come to light and undermine the "new map".

Allow yourself to imagine new figures who represent the people whose support you needed back then, in the past. These ideal figures, imagined in the appropriate situations, will create effective "new memories" to antidote the negative effect of the origins of the Inner Critic.

You are looking to imagine the perfect opposite of the person who caused the original problem. So a "Critical Community Member" might be effectively antidoted by a "Friendly Community Member" – who would have encouraged you. Other popular Inner Coach antidotes have included a bully on the playground – antidoted by a "Good Friend who helps you stand up for yourself"; an absent father – antidoted by an "Ideal Father who would have been there whenever you needed him"; and an angry mother – antidoted by an "Ideal Mother who would have loved you just as you are".

Some people feel a sense of disloyalty in imagining new friends or parents. The exercise is not in any way intended to blame actual figures from your past, but simply to counteract whatever effect you are still carrying within you. We would encourage you to try it. Remember it is not real, it is an image, but the image can help shape your future reality in a positive way. You are not actually replacing anyone, you are simply creating a new, more positive image, to give you a new, more positive message to create a new, more positive "memory" to help your presentations.

Exercise 4h: Imagining an Inner Coach – Level 2

This exercise will take 10–20 minutes, undisturbed, with your journal and pen at hand. Read each section until you are clear about the task, then begin.

i) Relax. Practise a little gentle, deep breathing. Allow the words you created as an antidote to come into your mind. What tone of voice do you hear these words in? Who is it that you would have wanted to say these words to you, back then? Allow an image of this person or ideal Inner Coach to form in your mind. Look at their face, examine their features. What role are they playing for you? Name it for yourself and name the positive effect they would have had, if they had been there, back then. Hear them saying the antidote message again. Allow yourself to take it in and believe it. Be aware of how this makes you feel.

ii) Think about how your life (and presentations) would have been different if you had heard these words from this figure, instead of experiencing the origin of the Inner Critic.

iii) Make some notes about the figure you imagined. What would you call them? How did they appear? How did they sound? How did you feel?

Now you have the right words and the right figure available, it is time to put them to work.

USING THE INNER COACH – LEVEL 2

Exercises 4g) and h) are the building blocks for the next exercise so please make sure you have completed them before moving on to 4i).

Exercise 4i: Active Imagination to Summon the Inner Coach – Level 2

The following exercise will take about 15–20 minutes, undisturbed, with your journal and pen at hand. It is an Active Imagination exercise. Be patient and don't rush it. It may take a few tries to get all the way through to a positive result. Read the instructions a few times until you are clear about what you will be doing, then start when you are ready. (You may wish to have a blanket and/or cushions available as props for section iii.)

i) You will need to find an appropriate place to sit or stand to imagine you are back in the original situation that was the root cause of the development of the Inner Critic. Close your eyes. Find a body posture for yourself appropriate to the original memory. Imagine the place you were originally in and what happened and/or the people who spoke to you. Remember what they said and feel the effect it had on you. Acknowledging the feeling is important here, even if it is uncomfortable.

ii) Now summon up your ideal Inner Coach. Remember their positive role in relation to you. Remember what they look like and place them – in your mind's eye – where you most want them in this situation. Take the time to really imagine them being present with you back then. Now allow them to speak their antidote to you – let it sink in – and register any impact this has on you.

iii) Begin to make a "body memory" of the feeling. Imagine you are able to take a photographic record of how you feel with the Inner Coach present. If you feel the support somewhere specific in your body (eg chest, stomach, back of the neck) gently place a hand there to reinforce the feeling with a physical sensation. If you want support in a place you cannot comfortably reach, move about or use props (leaning against a wall, sitting on cushions etc) to reinforce the feeling. When it feels right, allow the Inner Coach to speak again. Really take in the message, as deeply as you can. Let it sink deep into the core of your being, reinforced by the physical sensation you have created to support the message. Allow yourself to believe what the Inner Coach is saying. Trust that they know you, they support you and they wish you well.

iv) Now, secure in your knowledge of the support from the Inner Coach, imagine the impact they would have had on the original situation. They would have helped you create a very different assumption. If there was a negative figure present, they might have silenced them, diminished their power or reduced them in some way – maybe even causing them to double up or fall to the ground. Use your imagination to create the result that fits you. Continue imagining the Coach's voice and words antidoting the situation until there is no negative impact for you in it.

v) Now let the Inner Coach speak again, reinforced by the physical sensation you have created to support the message. Imagine taking a picture of this new scene, with the figure of the Inner Coach present and giving support to you, and store it in your memory bank. Know that you will be able to draw on this new picture whenever you need to. Let it sink in, as if it were penetrating your very bones. Imagine how your life and expectations of the future might have been different if this Coach had been present with you back then. Let this alternative reality sink in – because this possibility is open to you now. Imagine what it would have been like to grow up – from the age of your original memory right up to the present – with this voice as your Coach and support. Take your time with this. Internalize it as much as you can. Then, when you are ready, let the picture go and relax.

vi) When you are ready, write down your experience in your journal. This will reinforce the experience, and add weight to the "new memory" you have just created.

Some people even like to draw an image of the Inner Coach, to make the figure more Present for them. When you have this new figure available in your image memory bank you can call on it whenever you wish. The more you summon the Inner Coach the more you reinforce the positive "new memory", and the sooner you build up the "new map".

Exercise 4j: Summoning the Inner Coach for a Presentation – Level 2

i) Next time you know you will be entering a situation likely to trigger the Inner Critic, prepare yourself. If you can, go into the relevant room some time before the meeting/presentation is due to begin. Find the spot you will be sitting in and/or speaking from. Settle, breathe and ground yourself. Now imagine the Inner Coach being with you, in the appropriate place and speaking their words to you. Try and re-connect to the feeling you had in your Active Imagination rehearsal. Now imagine that your audience is in the room and the Inner Coach is still there, still supporting you. Let the Inner Coach speak to you again. Feel the added re-assurance this gives. Repeat as much of this as you can when the meeting/presentation actually starts. Especially if the Inner Critic shows up, simply take a deep breath and let the Inner Coach antidote their words. Remember how the Inner Coach can help you and how they can diminish the impact of a negative situation or voice. Let them do their work

OR

ii) If you cannot actually get to "rehearse" in the room beforehand, simply find your own time and place to rehearse in your head. Bring the image of the Inner Coach into your mind's eye. This could be in your office, in the washroom or even through simply practising inner attention – and withdrawing some of your energy inside at any time. If you don't have any other options, you can even imagine your rehearsal while sitting in the room waiting for your time to speak.

iii) If there is a trusted colleague in the audience ask them afterwards for feedback. Did you come across more confidently etc?

iv) Make notes in your journal. What difference did the Inner Coach make? Did the antidote work? If so, keep going with this Inner Coach and these words. If not, repeat whatever steps are necessary until you create the ideal Inner Coach for you.

We recommend that you work with these "Inner Coach" exercises for a while, over the course of a few weeks at least. Be patient; if these concepts are unfamiliar it may take a while for you to integrate them and recognize their value. If, during or after your engagement with Level 1 or 2, you wish to reinforce the learning with others present in a live situation you can find relevant information on presentation coaching in Further Resources. Otherwise, when you have overcome some of your blocks to confident performance, it is time to start expanding your repertoire...

PART 3

Expanding the Repertoire

Chapter 5

Playing the Right Character

Now we have examined the foundations and the blocks to confident performance, it is time to explore new possibilities. In theatre a good actor is versatile. They can play many different characters in many different ways. An effective acting training will encourage us to expand our repertoire and enlarge the range of our potential performance. Peak performers do not rely on one trick, or one style of delivery; they have a selection at their disposal and much of their talent is exercised in choosing the right style for the right moment.

In Shakespeare's play *Hamlet* he has his lead character say to a group of travelling players; "Suit the action to the word, the word to the action..." (Act 3 Scene 2). He is saying that if you deliver the right words with the wrong actions you will not have the impact you desire. The same is true of presentations. If you wish to maximize your impact you will need to think through your presentation task, assess your (and others') intentions and explore the range of "characters" available to you in order to achieve those intentions. These are the tasks we will learn how to complete in this Part of the book.

DIFFERENTIATING ROLE AND PERSONALITY

Expanding your repertoire is not about faking it, or pretending to be someone else. It is about assessing the requirements of the role you have been assigned and working out how you can best meet the role requirements. You will need to marry the external role to your internal personality if you truly wish to "suit the action to the word".

All good performance has a truthful quality to it, but often the best performance has an edge to it; the performer is pushing outside of their comfort zone, not being safe, is taking a risk – and thereby engaging our full attention. Of course, you do not have to expand your repertoire to anything like the range required of a professional actor, but the techniques we will use to expand your presentation potential are essentially the same.

During this Part of the book we will be deliberately working "outside-in", the more typically traditional English approach to acting. We will explore the different characters you may need to play and help you learn to play those characters convincingly. Later, in the "Authenticity" chapter, we will learn the more typically American approach, "inside-out", where you will be encouraged to find a personal, emotional connection to your presentation subject. Once you have mastered both "outside-in" and "inside-out" you will have a powerful range of tools available to help you.

"Outside-in" considers first the external reality. What is the effect you want to have on your audience, and what character do you need to play to achieve that effect? Different desired outcomes require different styles (and content) of performance. The ability to shift "character" to fit the situation will give you a versatility you previously did not think likely or possible.

INTRODUCING THE CHARACTERS

The characters we work with are drawn from the field of archetypal psychology (see figure opposite). We call them the Good King, the Great Mother, the Medicine Woman and the Warrior.

Originally based on the work of Carl Jung, and expanded by James Hillman, Robert Moore, Gareth Hill and others, the field of archetypal psychology has extensively investigated the underlying energetic drives of human beings. Research shows that most of us orientate ourselves around a principal priority from each of two pairs of opposing stances – Static or Dynamic, Masculine or Feminine (the latter are not gender specific but lie as potentials within each woman or man, much like the Yin and Yang of Eastern philosophy).

The Dynamic takes risks, moves forward into the unknown and is adaptable, whereas the Static seeks stability, consolidates the known and is generally conservative in outlook. The Masculine concentrates on doing;

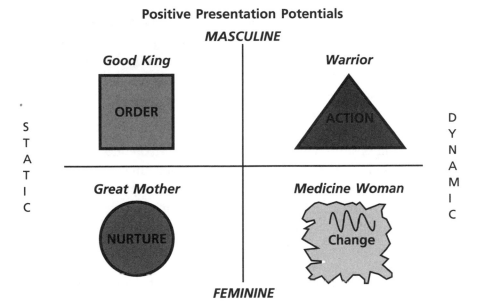

Positive Presentation Potentials

task, planning and implementation – "the What, the How and the When" – whereas the Feminine focuses more on being; creation, meaning and relationship – "the Who and the Why".

When these two preferences combine they create a character choice that we tend to favour as we meet the challenges of our work and world. Just as an actor may particularly enjoy a certain type of part (villain, hero, lover, funny friend etc) so we tend to prefer certain roles we are asked to play at work. This inevitably comes out in the way we present ourselves to others, in both informal and formal settings, whether it be a one-to-one briefing or an international conference.

IDENTIFYING YOUR FAVOURITE CHARACTER

As you read the following try to get a sense of your personal favourite. Given the choice and the opportunity, which of these do you prefer to play/be at work?

When the Static and the Masculine energies meet they combine to produce the character of the Good King. He or she creates order through rational strategic processes. They assess the past with detailed analysis, collect information, maintain an objective overview and suggest plans for sensible development. They hold their place with authority, communicate with weight and gravitas, and "bless" others with appropriate praise and recognition.

When the Static and Feminine energies meet they combine to produce the Great Mother. These are "people people". They value and support others, offer protection and build trust. They see people for who they really are and wish to develop them to their full potential. They thrive on relationships, welcome informal conversation and act as bonding agents and networkers within teams. They open channels of communication and genuinely care for their people.

When the Dynamic and the Feminine energies meet they combine to produce the Medicine Woman. These people are naturally creative, spontaneous and innovative. They embrace change as an exciting opportunity for renewal. They dream and intuit the future, they paint pictures with words. They create metaphors that allow others to see the present from a new perspective.

And last but not least, when the Dynamic and the Masculine energies meet they produce the Warrior. These are the heroes and heroines who love to achieve the goal. They inspire themselves and others into action, to do the best that they can do. They regularly motivate their people and set demanding targets. They assert themselves forcefully in their attempts to "make the grade" and to win.

Four very different characters which all offer positive qualities and skills for your future presentations. Everyone has the potential to play all four characters, but most of us tend to use some more than others. Life choices and career development often lead us to prioritize those that have first "worked" for us and got us recognized. Which means, of course, that most of us have one or two characters that we tend not to play as much.

If you haven't done so already, use the following chart to try and identify your favourite and your least favourite of the four characters.

All four characters have gifts and effective attributes to offer a presentation. As we move through the next four chapters we will give you more details about what each character has to offer, and ideas and

Character Qualities

GOOD KING

Static Masculine

Sets objectives	Deliberate
Praises success	Precise
Informative	Methodical
Recognizes effort	Analytical
Authoratitive	Logical
Controlling influence	Assesses
Attends to detail	Practical

WARRIOR

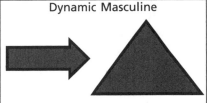

Dynamic Masculine

Inspiring	Motivating
Persuasive	Forceful
Sells vision	Task focused
Competitive	Gives a "call to arms"
Strong willed	Rousing
Confident	Instils belief
Challenging	Confronts

GREAT MOTHER

Static Feminine

Reassuring	Encouraging
Supportive	Empathetic
Responsive	Sharing
Helpful	Relaxed
Relational	Welcoming
Receptive	Builds trust
Radiates warmth	Develops others

MEDICINE WOMAN

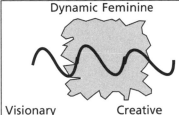

Dynamic Feminine

Visionary	Creative
Creates change	Adaptable
Enthusiastic	Demonstrative
"Sparky"	Animated
Imaginative	Inspired
Paints pictures	Dynamic
(with words)	Experimental

techniques that will enable you to learn to play all four, as necessary. This is important because if we do not expand our range we can get stuck in our favourite role. Just as certain actors get type-cast, and are rarely considered for roles outside that type, so we can get attached to a certain role at work, and find it difficult to be taken seriously outside of that mould.

OVERPLAYING YOUR FAVOURITE CHARACTER

What we have seen consistently over the years is that many presenters undermine their message by overplaying their "favourite character". Often, we find, it is one of their less favourite characters that will actually best meet the current presentation challenge.

Those who need to confront unacceptable behaviour (which best suits the Warrior) but prefer to support others (Great Mother) often make the mistake of smiling a warm welcome to the group. This gives the message "Thank you so much for coming – how nice to see you…", which severely undermines the tough stance required for people to feel confronted about their behaviour.

On the other hand, some habitual Warriors may need to call an open Q & A or feedback session but then look at their watch every two minutes, creating the impression that they don't really want to be there, wasting "valuable time". Good Kings might ask people to be more creative and innovative in their approach but then demand a clear budget and implementation schedule before listening to a new idea, which usually kills the creative spark. And Medicine Women may be tempted to call a brainstorm session during a crisis while what others really need is a clear list of priorities. The fact is that when we get stuck playing our favourite character we often begin to invoke its negative potential.

If we never leave the place occupied by our favourite character, or if we always return to it as soon as possible, we will eventually appear to those around us to be turning into the negative version of the positive potential. And if we keep going in this manner long enough we *will* turn into the negative. It is possible to have too much of a good thing!

REHEARSING A NEW CHARACTER

Many managers have been promoted to their current level of responsibility precisely because they play one or two of the characters really well. But if we wish to achieve Peak Performance we need to learn to play all four – well enough. So how can we do it?

The answer, as is true for most ideas in this book, lies in the simple process of Awareness, Rehearsal and Reflection. Until we are aware of what characters we tend to play, and tend not to play, there is no motivation to change. Once we have awareness, we need to practise playing the new desired character to build experience. And then we need to reflect upon what we did, how it worked, and what we might want to try differently next time.

If we don't try it we will never be able to do it, but if we first try it under the pressure of a real work presentation then we engage in a high risk strategy. Would a good actor ever step onto a stage for a first night performance without preparation and rehearsal? Would a professional sports person ever step onto a field without training and warming up first? Not unless some crisis demanded it. Preparation and rehearsal are essential.

Some people ask; "Why not just stick to the character you are good at playing?" To which we reply; "Why not add more strings to your bow, particularly when you realize the limitation of only playing one or two characters?" Learning to play other characters will not in any way lessen your ability to continue playing the one you are best at. But it *will* give you more options, and enable you to meet a wide range of presentation situations much more effectively.

During the next four chapters we will uncover the depth of what each character offers a presentation. We will assess what they offer your preparation, as well as your performance. We will think about what might stop you playing a particular character, some of the personal and cultural voices that may currently inhibit you, and give you rehearsal exercises to bring the desired character closer. We will finish each chapter with a list of activities that you can practise outside of work which will give you experience of getting into the appropriate energy without the pressure of performance. We encourage you to work through all four characters; even though you will be repeating some exercises you will be applying them to different characters, and gaining different insights.

We advise you to rehearse the characters by yourself for a while, to get the feel of the character and give yourself time to learn. One of the great things about a theatre rehearsal room is that there is no failure, only learning opportunities. No good actor can ever learn the best way to play a new character by getting it right all the time. You have to stretch, play, extend and sometimes go too far in order to get the feel of what might be right, for you.

When you have rehearsed and you feel ready, seek feedback. In between rehearsal and performance a more objective opinion can be invaluable. Just as the actor has a director and a sports person has a coach, we advise you to find a trusted feedback source to try your "new character" out on, before you take it into a real presentation. We can use friends or colleagues – if we trust their judgement – or a professional coach if resources permit (see Further Resources p. 221).

In our courses we spend a good amount of time in rehearsal, coaching participants as they learn to play their less favourite characters. We have distilled their learning into the next four chapters. As you will see, all four characters have their key attitudes and behaviours that also translate into body language, gesture, vocal tone and use of distinct language. With appropriate rehearsal, all these can be yours!

Chapter 6

The Good King – Order and Authority

The Good King embodies an ordered, measured world-view. He communicates with weight and gravitas, and exudes inner authority. His presence has a calm, statesmanlike quality with which he delivers an overview of a situation, an assessment of figures or details of some important information or new strategy. Where appropriate, he praises people and acknowledges success. When we see a speaker with these qualities we are likely to trust and respect him. In a time of crisis we will feel safe under his stewardship.

We start with the Good King because this character also has the most to offer the analysis and preparation of your presentation material. His methodical nature comes to the fore. Strategic identification of key objectives, details and careful planning are all within his gift. Even if you do not need the Good King in the presentation itself, you will certainly need him in your preparation.

PART 1 – THE GOOD KING PREPARES

Any effective acting training programme will teach potential performers how to address key preparation issues during rehearsal. As we said in the Introduction, we are not primarily concerned with tailoring the detailed content of your presentation but rather with giving you tools drawn from performance culture with which to approach your presentation in a new and more interesting way. From our years in rehearsal rooms and acting training we have distilled what we feel are the most useful approaches to preparation. These are:

1 Find a Super Objective – clarify and define a clear goal.

2 Assess the audience – know to whom you are talking and their current reality or mood.

3 Discover personal motivation – identify why you want to achieve your Super Objective with this audience.

4 Analyse the role requirement – decide which role you need to play.

5 Rehearse the role – practise how you are going to play the desired role and make adjustments.

Those of you already dreading the prospect of "homework" have probably got something to learn from the Good King. He researches his subject matter and prepares his material.

You will need a presentation subject to rehearse these elements of preparation. If you have a real upcoming presentation, so much the better; if not, pick a subject you would typically be asked to present on – past, present or future – and imagine a typical audience for it. Use this as your test subject throughout the exercises on preparation. Even if you never actually give this presentation, the fact that you have applied these techniques once will make them easier for you to use in the future. Inevitably some people will find some parts of this preparation toolkit more useful and effective than others. We encourage you to do it all at least once, and then select the exercises that help you the most.

SUPER OBJECTIVE – FINDING THE "WHY"

Why are you going to present? What do you want to achieve? Can you identify the overarching goal of the whole presentation?

All effective presentations have a desired outcome in mind. Just as no serious sports professional would go out on a field without having a clear goal in mind, no decent actor will enter a stage without knowing what their character wants from the scene they are entering. This is what we call the "Super Objective", the over-arching goal. Ideally you should know not only what you want as presenter but also the desired outcome for the audience. And, we would argue, that if you are not trying to change something in your audience then don't bother – send them an e-mail.

Remember that sharing information is not particularly inspiring. If this is your goal we would ask you to think carefully about what exactly are the key messages you want to impart. Humans retain information much better when they read it than when they listen to it. Why do you want to talk to them about this? Why not just let them read it?

Keep checking your motives and your goals. Don't try and do too much in a single presentation. Better to keep it short and leave them wanting more than to inflict "death by PowerPoint" on your captive audience.

What is the one big thing that you want to change in your audience? What is it that they currently think or do that you want to change?

These are the questions that help actors and directors find the Super Objective. The clearer you are about your Super Objective, the more likely it will be that you can create the right strategies to deliver it.

> Richard was asked to give a talk to a group of senior civil servants undergoing a large-scale change initiative in their department:
>
> "I had several conversations with different senior managers after which I was swamped with several possible and differing objectives. These included 'Giving them a new perspective', 'Rewarding the effort so far', 'Learning how to engage others in the change process more fully', 'Realizing where they were failing their staff' and 'Learning new behaviours to counter the negative comments from a recent management survey'. All well and good, and useful briefing material, except that if I simply followed instructions and put a talk together to meet all of these valid interests it would end up a mess, and fall between several stools on the way. Finally I went back to the HR Director with a proposal for a single, unifying Super Objective – 'Engaging ourselves and others in change' – which seemed to me to meet many of the potential objectives while providing an overarching frame to design a presentation around. Once this was agreed I could concentrate my efforts to ensure that everything I said and did was aimed at achieving this goal."

Once you have a defined and agreed a Super Objective you have your priority clear and know what you want to change in the audience. We advise you to find and use *active* verbs when possible. When the Super Objective is active you have something to pursue. "Engaging ourselves and others in change" is more active than "Realizing where we are failing our staff"; "Blowing apart complacency" is better than "Informing them about the competition's growth rate"; "Welcoming new staff" has more heart than "Newcomers' introductory talk"; "Selling the Vision" is more direct than "Sharing next year's business plan". Now it's your turn.

Exercise 6a: Defining the Super Objective

i) Pick a presentation subject – real or imagined; make a few notes as to the big themes it will cover.

ii) Make a list of all the reasons you can think of to give this presentation.

iii) What is it you most want to change in your audience's current thinking or activity?

iv) Look through the list and see if you can "activate" any of these potential objectives by reframing them with a more active verb or phrase.

v) Now see where the energy is. Which ones are the most active in intent and most likely to engage you as the speaker? Now choose the most active overall intention that doesn't contradict any of the key (or non-negotiable) objectives.

This is now your Super Objective. This, for us, is the beginning – the "Why". Now we will move on to the "Who".

ASSESSING THE AUDIENCE – THE "WHO"

Who are they? And what's on their mind?

Different constituents, stakeholders or groups of employees are best addressed in different ways. It is a naïve actor (and speaker) who approaches each audience as if it were the same. The more you know, or can realistically imagine, about your audience the better. When you know who they are, what are their concerns and what they might need to hear from you in order for you to achieve your Super Objective, you are much more likely to truly engage them. Even if it is a very mixed audience then that's good to know; you may need several strategies or characters in performance to engage the different parts.

If you realize that you have no idea what a particular part of the audience may be thinking, but you know that they hold an important key to achieving your goal, it may be time for a few confidential chats, a focus group or even a staff survey.

If you can add an effective audience assessment to your Super Objective you will begin to understand not only what you want but also how you may need to go about getting it.

We worked with the Executive Team of a major communications company that was two years past a large merger. The team had recently commissioned an employee survey that revealed considerable dislocation between the different pre-merger entities and a general perception of a lack of visible leadership. The Executive Team were due to speak to their employees in a few days to respond to the identified concerns. We worked with them to prepare effective presentations. They identified their Super Objective as "Uniting our people through visible leadership". They assessed their audience and agreed that the current mindset of "not belonging" was the biggest point of change they needed to achieve.

Now they were able to brainstorm ideas about what people would need to hear from them in order to feel more united in the future. The company had retained pre-merger division names and added a new layer to manage the whole. People didn't want to lose their identity in an anonymous whole, they wanted to feel part of it. As the Executive Team's ideas were refined the theme of "family" began to emerge. The new layer could be seen as the "family name" – that which binds them together – and the old names were equivalent to first names, which establish individual identity. This image could serve both to overcome the apparent dislocation and – if it was delivered well – would exhibit visible leadership. This became the overarching theme of the presentations we then went on to rehearse – and it emerged from a careful assessment of the audience.

We invite you to spend some time on the following exercises and see what answers you come up with. You may not be able to answer all the questions for every part of the audience, but the more information you have the more focus you can achieve in delivery.

Exercise 6b: Audience Assessment

i) Who will you be talking to? List as many potentially different constituents of your audience as you can. This may be a broad range (eg from temporary

support staff all the way up to permanent board members) or a narrow range (eg established shop floor team leaders and newer shop floor team leaders).
ii) What is the general mood? List the primary moods or the likely range of moods – anxious, confident, bullish, fearful, complacent etc.
iii) What is on their mind? List your audience's primary concerns right now – a recent bad report, supply lines, interest rates, survival, football, shopping, children etc.
iv) What in their current mindset do you most need to break down or break through in order to achieve your Super Objective? Make a list from your experience and/or your best guess – "We've got it all", "We're unassailable", "We're doomed", "I'd better watch out for Number One!", "Management never listens to us" etc.
v) If you were in their shoes, what would you need to hear in order for the Super Objective to be achieved? Some Active Imagination can be useful here. Imagine that you are in their position. What might shift their current mindset? Write down anything you think remotely useful. Try not to censor yourself. From some of the apparently most ludicrous first thoughts can come the most effective final ideas.
vi) Refine the option – mark the constituents, moods, mindsets, statements and ideas that feel the most relevant.

MOTIVATION – WHY DO YOU WANT IT?

Your personal motivation to achieve a desired goal is what will give your presentation some "juice". Knowing why you want something helps you move towards achieving it. If there is nothing in it for you, chances are the audience won't care either.

What motivates you to achieve the desired goal? What's in it for you?

This may sound selfish, but it is important, especially if you have to make the same presentation a number of times. You will have to keep it fresh. Knowing why you want to achieve the Super Objective is a motivational key. You may have to bring it clearly into your mind before you set foot on the platform or in front of the boardroom table.

We worked with a large European reinsurance company's senior management development programme. The company was facing a large and potentially ruinous US lawsuit and a new American manager had to try and convince the conservative board of the necessity of entering a publicity battle for the hearts and minds of the public. The Super Objective was clear. This audience of board members would, he knew, be resistant to his suggestion. In the face of this resistance he was feeling over-awed at the task in hand. What could he possibly say that might sway them? We explained to him that if he could find what really motivated him to achieve his Super Objective then he would have a platform from which to begin. It couldn't guarantee his desired outcome but it would give him the right internal commitment to try his best. We asked him to sit down and think about why he personally thought this was important, on several levels. What was in it for him? What did he think was in it for his company? And why might this be good for the world?

He worked on these questions for a while and then came back to us. Personally, he believed in fair play; the plaintiff in the lawsuit was putting out unbalanced and negative reports about the company and he was personally motivated to try and redress the balance. Organizationally, survival was at stake. If the lawsuit were lost it would have huge ramifications for thousands of employees and clients. Finally, on a global level, the world could lose an institution that helped others rebuild after tragedy.

Even as he named these motivations for speaking his energy changed. It was as if someone had switched on a light. He was already looking and sounding more confident and committed to achieving his goal. This was the motivation he needed to brave the poker-faced board the next day. He had found his "Why me?"

So, what's yours? Of course it may change from presentation to presentation and from job to job. All the more reason to keep asking the questions.

Exercise 6c: Finding Motivation

i) What motivates you personally about achieving the goal? ("What's in it for me?")

ii) Why is this important for the team/department/organization? ("What's in it for us?")

iii) What is this serving in the bigger picture? How might it make the community in which we work and/or the world in which we live a better place?

The following story is almost certainly apocryphal, but nonetheless makes a valuable point.

> When Christopher Wren was supervising the construction of St Paul's Cathedral in London he once spoke to four bricklayers, all constructing the same wall, to check that they understood their task. "What are you doing?" he asked the first worker; "What I get paid for – putting sticky stuff on bricks" came the honest reply. He asked the second worker the same question; "I'm building a wall." On to number three; "I'm helping build a cathedral." And finally the fourth; "I'm part of a huge community building a cathedral, for the glory of God."

The fourth bricklayer is likely to have the most access to motivation because he has connected his personal job – sticky stuff on bricks – through the current team task – building a wall – to the organizational goal – constructing a cathedral – to a higher purpose – honouring the glory of God. Whereas the first bricklayer is likely to get demotivated if the sticky stuff doesn't stick right, and the second demotivated if the wall he is creating is deemed superfluous to the building, number four has ever higher levels of motivation available to him. The more levels you have, the more personal resource you have access to. The more important you make the presentation for yourself, the more impact it will have on others.

ROLE ANALYSIS

Now, having done the groundwork and investigated your Super Objective, audience and motivation, you are now ready to decide which character or characters will best fit the task at hand. What role does this presentation demand? Is it closer to Good King, Great Mother, Medicine Woman or Warrior? The lists opposite should help you to at least narrow down the possibilities.

Presentation Roles

GOOD KING

Static Masculine

Assesses the past	Sets objectives
Admonishes bad practice	Uses logic
Accepts responsibility	Praises success
Delivers information	Is methodical
Recognizes effort	Analyses results
Calms in a crisis	Exudes authority
Is practical	Attends to detail

WARRIOR

Dynamic Masculine

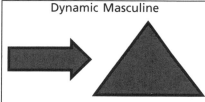

Sells vision	Motivates others
Instils belief	Confronts complacency
Focuses on results	Encourages competition
Rouses passion	Uses forceful persuasion
Exudes confidence	Sets tough targets
Gives a"call to arms"	Exudes will-power
Is inspiring	Challenges people to win

GREAT MOTHER

Static Feminine

Welcomes new people	Builds trust
Reassures in tough times	Offers support
Exudes positive feeling	Radiates warmth
Responds to concerns	Shares best practice
Is relaxed and helpful	Creates open culture
Demonstrates empathy	Is receptive
Encourages participation	Develops others

MEDICINE WOMAN

Dynamic Feminine

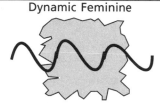

Imagines the future	Creates vision
Paints pictures	Uses metaphor
Dares to dream	Is enthusiastic
Animates others	Inspires the new
Creates change	Excites possibilities
Brainstorms	Dynamic
Sparks "out of the box" thinking	Encourages adaptability

One character may suffice for a simple presentation, whereas more complex or diverse subjects may require more than one character. You may be able to divide the subjects between the characters. Welcoming people (Great Mother), analysing results (Good King), setting a tough target (Warrior) and painting a bright picture of a better future (Medicine Woman). Generally though, we would advise against trying to do too much or be all things to all people in a single presentation. Often, instead of getting three or four messages clearly, people hear a mixed message, which confuses them.

Another common problem is that there are some messages that some people find extremely hard to deliver well. While most of us are comfortable delivering messages most closely associated with our favourite character, many of us have trouble delivering messages that relate more closely to our least favourite character. This is often where our greatest learning lies, and it is often in this character than we can most usefully learn to expand our repertoire. The key is to be able to push the edge of our comfort zone but still be believable to ourselves, and others.

Richard was directing Mark Rylance as Henry V for the opening of Shakespeare's Globe Theatre in London:

"Mark is a wonderful, sensitive and creative actor, but not naturally heroic in style. Henry V is traditionally depicted as the archetypal warrior hero, all blood and guts urging everyone 'Once more unto the breach...' If Mark simply played the character as himself he would not do the part and the words justice, but if he faked it and put on a heroic act he did not believe in then he would not be able to play it with integrity. One of my jobs, through the rehearsal process, was to enable Mark to find the right "marriage" between role and personality – so he could fulfil the role with integrity. In the end he created a fascinating study of a sensitive new King, learning how to be what his people needed to see, in order to achieve what he needed them to do. His was a Henry V who recognized that an effective leader also needs to be an effective actor. The unique combination of character and personality made a compelling performance."

So, some presentations will naturally fall within the remit of your favourite character, while others will not. The presentations that require you to embody your least favourite character will be the most difficult for you to perform well. It is not impossible, but it will take more preparation and thought. The first step is awareness. What is your favourite character? If it is different from what is required in a particular presentation it is worth planning how you can combine the two effectively. If the required character is a difficult one for you to play convincingly, being honest about it is sometimes the best way forward.

We worked with a senior manager from the financial sector who had come out of the US Marine Corps. Not surprisingly, he was most comfortable playing the Warrior, motivating others to make more effort and leading by example. During his coaching session he had identified that the Great Mother was his least favourite position. But, a couple of weeks after the course, he found himself facing an intensely difficult situation. His company had, tragically, occupied two floors of the World Trade Center. On the morning of 12 September 2001, he had to face his staff in the London office. He sat up late the night before trying to think how he could best address the situation. Having worked with the characters he was aware that his habitual Warrior response would have been along the lines of "All right folks, a terrible thing has happened, but we can't do anything about it over here so let's get back to work and make sure we meet our targets this month." But he now recognized that what would have been most comfortable for him personally was not necessarily the most appropriate character role to meet the current situation. He assessed the audience and their likely state of mind and thought about what his people might need from him. He decided to try and play more of the Great Mother role but, having analysed that this was his least favourite character, he knew that it would be difficult. Eventually he came up with a strategy – honesty. The next morning he gathered all his people together and began:

"Listen guys, you know me. What I would most like to do right now would be to tell you all that there is nothing we can do about the tragic events of yesterday and that we should get back to work ASAP. But maybe that is not the right thing to do now. So I thought I'd call you all together and see what you want to do." He reported that, after a brief silence, people began to open up about their feelings, their sense of loss, grief and helplessness. The meeting lasted all morning, but when it finished everyone felt heard and supported and ready to do what needed to be done. He had indeed been able to hold the space occupied by the Great Mother, but – crucially – he had done it with honesty and integrity. He had not pretended to be someone else but had opened up to the possibility that his favourite character was not best suited to the role this situation required. One of his staff said it was one of the best examples of crisis management she had ever seen.

Exercise 6d: Role Analysis

i) Bearing in mind your Super Objective and audience assessment, which character is most required for this presentation?
ii) If different from your favourite character, what might you need to be aware of? How might your favourite character undermine this presentation?

You may need to rehearse playing a least favourite character before you are ready to go into the next exercise. We will explore rehearsing the characters and overcoming potential obstacles within each. Those that apply to the Good King start after "Rehearsal with Feedback" below, which will complete our overview of effective preparation of presentation material.

REHEARSAL WITH FEEDBACK

Those readers who enjoy seeing classic pieces of theatre, dance or music will be aware that the same piece of work can be interpreted in many different ways, some better than others. If you see a lot, every so often you'll see a bad show. Someone whose interpretation of the piece is so at odds with how you imagine it that you can hardly bear to sit through it. This happens with presentations too.

If you have gone through all the other stages of preparation, it is time to figure out this last piece of the puzzle – how you can best play the role to achieve the Super Objective with this audience.

We were coaching a senior manager in a European division of a global fast food company. This manager had researched Corporate Social Responsibility (CSR) initiatives and ecological studies and wanted his company to get more involved in these approaches. He had fought for and won the right to address the board at their next meeting. He did his homework and decided that the Good King was the right role, but when we saw his first rehearsal we realized that he was not going to get very far. He was coming across as the authoritarian Good King, laying down the law and telling the board what they were doing wrong; "Do you realize the damage some of the by-products of our industry are producing in the environment? It is our responsibility to get our act together and do something about it." Even though he may have been completely right in his accusation, it was extremely unlikely that the board would want to listen to his suggestions. He was making them feel wrong and talked down to. He was not playing the character in the right way. We asked him to imagine being in the shoes of the board members, and think what they would need to hear in order to do what he wanted them to do. He got some ideas, jotted down some notes and then started again. After another rehearsal his pitch began something like this:

"Are you aware of how many of our regular customers are taking an active interest in the environmental effect of the products they consume? And how many consumers are now saying that they will actively consider the CSR stance of companies they regularly buy from? And by what percentage this CSR inclined consumer is estimated to grow over the next five years? If we invest in developing a sustainable packaging process now I believe we will gain a substantial advantage over our competitors within the next five years..." Now we felt he would get their attention and their interest. He was still using Good King gifts – information, analysis, projections etc – but was presenting in a way his audience would be more inclined to listen to.

A good way in to this "How" is to ask yourself: "If I were in their shoes what would I need to hear?" This is a simple but vital step, away from simply "What do I want to say?" to "What do they need to hear?"

Exercise 6e: Rehearsal with Feedback

Before you complete this exercise you should make some notes on what you want to say and ask a colleague whose opinion you trust to help you.
i) Set the scene; tell them who you are going to be talking to and what your goal in giving this presentation is. Ask them to imagine that they are the intended audience.
ii) Go through your presentation.
iii) Get feedback. Would they have wanted to listen to you? Did you

achieve your goal? What else might this audience need to hear in order for your goal to be achieved?

iv) Go through your presentation again with any suggested additions and amendments.

v) Get feedback.

vi) Continue this process of rehearsal and feedback until you have refined your material successfully.

The value of rehearsal is that you can practise and learn from potential mistakes before you stand in front of the audience. Once you have got it right, your mind and body will be much more likely to perform well under the pressure of actual performance.

Of course, not every presentation requires the level of preparation we suggest in this chapter. But, in general, the more tools and techniques you have at your disposal the better prepared you can be.

We often find that people who do not enjoy playing the Good King character under-prepare. They prefer to "wing it" and "see what comes out on the day" – sometimes this works, but sometimes it doesn't. So, if this is one of your less favourite characters, we suggest you pay more attention to preparation. You can always improvise around a prepared text if the mood takes you, but you can't stand up to wing it and then draw on preparation you haven't done.

A colleague of ours is a trial lawyer. When he goes in to sum up in front of a judge he has three options available to him. He has a fully written out speech that he can read if he is nervous or worried about forgetting important details. He has a one page summary that he can refer to while he is talking more off the cuff. Finally, he has a blank sheet of paper that he can put on top of all his notes if he is feeling particularly confident and inspired. If you have done the preparation then you have the choice.

PART 2 – PLAYING THE GOOD KING

If this character is a natural favourite of yours you may not need to engage in the exercises for the rest of this chapter, but we recommend you read through them in case there is something useful you are not currently considering when you play the Good King. Let's remind ourselves of the presentation gifts of this character. He or she:

Assesses the past
Sets objectives
Admonishes bad practice
Uses logic
Accepts responsibility
Praises success
Delivers information
Is methodical
Recognizes effort
Analyses results
Calms in a crisis
Exudes authority
Is practical
Attends to detail.

OBSTACLES

If this is one of your less favourite characters you might find some of these gifts difficult to access in your presentations. This is often due to a negative perception that you hold in your mind about the character. When you see someone at work for whom this is obviously a favourite character you may not immediately think of the gifts named above. You might just see the potential negatives first. These are what psychology calls "projections", the ideas we project onto other people because of our own personal preferences, experiences and history. Some of the typical negative projections about Good Kings include that they are: pedantic, boring, obsessive, controlling, dictatorial, committee-bound, focused on talk not action, over-focused on detail, prone to "analysis paralysis", rigid, pompous, arrogant, over-structured, resistant to change, hostile to emergent ideas, single-minded, over-critical, dull, uninspired, deadpan, stuck, predictable and blinkered.

This is not to say that you won't meet people who truly exhibit these negative tendencies, you will. But you may also find yourself projecting these negative judgements onto people who exhibit the gifts of the Good King. It is precisely because some of us do not recognize the positive potentials as gifts that we see the negative potentials first. As a result of this projection we naturally tend to avoid playing this character and we rarely, if ever, exhibit the behaviours that we dislike in others. The problem is that we also cut ourselves off from the *positive* potential of the character. The fact is that if you can recognize the negative potentials in others you are extremely unlikely to ever act out the negative side of the character yourself. It is the things that you are unaware of that you are likely to play out.

Most of us hold a negative projection about our least favourite character, and this is often an obstacle to us being able to embody this character well in presentations (as well as in the rest of our life). If we are to move through this obstacle we will need to identify the projections and, if we can, identify their origin.

These projections are another kind of inner critical voice, except this voice tends to criticize others rather than yourself. Unfortunately, this same voice often blocks our access to a character's gifts.

Susan had just been promoted to a senior management position at a Hong Kong bank. She came for coaching because she would now be required to make high level project presentations and she was experiencing a great deal of anxiety about this. She identified quickly that her new role required Good King energy and also realized that this was her least favourite role. We asked her to stand up and imagine herself as a regal Queen, confident of her intelligence and position. She tried for a moment and then stopped and said "I can't do it." As we coached her into figuring out what inner judgement she was making, she acknowledged a strong voice that said "You're being arrogant." We asked her to think about where this voice came from and she tracked it back to her childhood. She had grown up a very bright girl in a neighbourhood where girls "were not supposed to shine" intellectually. Whenever she exhibited her natural intelligence in front of family and/or friends her parents would tell her "You're being too opinionated, don't show off!" As she grew up she became much quieter around people in positions of authority.

When she went to work her first boss was very forthright with his opinions and she had thought him arrogant. She could now see that this projection, based on an old family voice, was stopping her inhabiting the natural authority of the Good King, just at the time when others wanted her intelligent opinions about important projects.

We did an Inner Coach exercise in which she found a Coach who validated her right to express her opinions – and did some Active Imagination work to give her access to positive images of the Good King. We then gave her some homework rehearsal exercises to practise playing this character. By the time we met her again, six weeks later, for a follow-up coaching day, she was able to stand up and speak with calm, intelligent authority. Once she had identified the projection and recognized where it came from she could move through it and into a better relationship with the Good King. Through rehearsal she was able to make the unfamiliar, familiar. Finally she was able to see, appreciate, practise and own the gifts of the character.

So, before we go into detail as to how you might want to rehearse playing the Good King, it would be helpful for you to know what obstacles might lie in your way.

Exercise 6f: Identifying Negative Projections about the Good King

This exercise will take 10–15 minutes with your journal at hand. We encourage you simply to read the questions in each numbered section and then write down your answers, without thinking too much about it. Just see what comes.

i) How would you describe your relationship to authority? How do you generally regard people who have formal authority over you? (These are usually people who have a prescribed right to tell you what to do and what not to do – judges, security forces, police, bank managers, local and national government officers etc.) Do you generally trust people who hold authority over you? If not, what do you usually think about them when you are in their presence and/or feeling their authority? Write without censoring yourself. Names, words, phrases, anything that comes to mind.

ii) What were your earliest memories of authority? Did authority come from parents, grandparents, other primary care givers, prefects, scout leaders, sports coaches, teachers, head teachers etc? Did you tend to respect those who laid out rules and regulations or did you tend to rebel against them?

iii) How do you feel about the authority that is exercised in your current place of work? Do you generally respect those managers and leaders who hold sway over you? If not, what do you think of them?

iv) Shut your eyes for a few seconds and imagine a figure of a King or Queen. What do you think about them? Would you trust this imagined figure?

v) Now read over and assess your answers to the above questions. Can you see a general pattern of response emerging?

vi) If so, is it clear where this pattern of projections came from? Like many inner voices, these may have started for excellent reasons. See if you can identify the causes of your current projections around authority and the Good King character. What in your life so far could be a cause of this pattern?

If you have found a strong critical voice you may wish to consider revisiting the "Inner Coach" chapter to find an antidote. If it feels manageable enough as it is, then try some of the rehearsal suggestions below.

A good first step is to find positive images of the Good King in your life, in history and in fiction. This will begin to build a positive pool of reference from which you will be able to draw in the future.

Exercise 6g: Finding Positive Images of the Good King

i) Personal role models – think of people that you personally know and respect, and who play this character well. Make a list of them and the qualities you admire in them.

ii) Public role models – think of people in the public eye, people whom you may never meet but whom you acknowledge to play the Good King well. They may be statesmen, world or local leaders, businessmen, politicians or spiritual leaders who you deem to be Good Kings and Queens. Some popular names in seminars have been: King Solomon, Nelson Mandela, Bill Clinton, Kofi Annan, Hans Blix, Colin Powell, Indira Gandhi, Madeline Allbright, Winston Churchill.

iii) Fictional role models – characters from works of fiction and/or the actors who play these parts particularly well: King Arthur, Martin Sheen in *The West Wing* etc.

If you find it really hard to come up with any positive examples in this exercise you may yet need to go back to the "Inner Coach" exercises in Chapter 4 to find positive reinforcement to enable you to start seeing the gifts of the Good King around you in the world. If you have some external images and resources you should be ready to find an internal image and resource. This can be accessed through an Active Imagination, or a guided "waking dream" (see below).

Exercise 6h: Active Imagination to Find the Good King

You will need 10–15 minutes undisturbed, with pen and paper, for this exercise. Read through the directions until you are familiar enough with the process to start by yourself – it is better to go all the way through the journey without stopping, if you can. Remember, this is an exercise about *imagination*.

i) Close your eyes and relax. Let all your thoughts and worries disappear. Imagine with your inner eye that you can now "levitate" your body. Imagine yourself floating upwards, moving through ceilings, floors and air as necessary until you are high in the sky. Now imagine yourself flying, very fast across landscapes and over water.

Now imagine an island on the horizon, coming closer. You land on the island, knowing there is a castle nearby, with a Good King inside, waiting to meet you. Imagine finding your way to the castle and meeting the Good King. Have a brief conversation; observe him carefully – how he holds himself, how he looks, how he acts.

When you are ready, take your leave and retrace your steps. Imagine flying back over water and landscapes until you arrive back in the room you started from. Stretch, open your eyes, and as soon as you are ready, write a record of your Active Imagination journey.

Note: To find the characters in these Active Imagination exercises we will invite you to imagine the archetypal gender associated with the character.

If you find this difficult or uncomfortable you are welcome to change the gender, from King to Queen, Medicine Woman to Magician etc.

Hopefully, by now you have a few different images of a Good King to work with. These are your resources to bring to rehearsal.

Exercise 6i: Rehearsal – Becoming the Image

This exercise is drawn from the work of the Russian teacher of acting, Michael Chekhov, nephew of the playwright Anton Chekhov. It will take you 10–15 minutes undisturbed in a room large enough to move about in and containing a straight-backed chair.

i) Look through your notes from 6g) and h). Select the image of a Good King that you feel to be the right one to rehearse "becoming" – you can always change your mind or try a few different ones later.

ii) Lie down on the floor and practise some diaphragm breathing. Relax and let your mind empty. When you are ready, see a corridor in your mind's eye, stretching out in front of you into the distance. Imagine that there is an entrance into the corridor at the far end where someone could enter into your line of vision. Know that the Good King you have chosen to work with is waiting just out of your sight, at the end of the corridor.

iii) When you are ready, "allow" the Good King to appear at the end of the corridor and let this figure begin to move towards you, maintaining their regal posture. Watch the figure carefully. Examine how they walk, how they move and how they hold themselves. Allow them to keep walking up to you until they are very close, imagine them greeting you and listen to how their voice sounds and their natural authority.

iv) When you are ready, imagine this figure turning round and backing into your actual body, as if it were a spirit entering a physical form. Imagine how your body would feel different if this figure were actually within you. How would it change the way you think, feel, move and talk?

v) When you are ready, allow yourself to get up and stand, as if you were now the figure. Try and feel the difference between how you stand now and how you normally stand. Allow yourself imaginatively to "become" the image, and practise moving about like the figure moved in your imagination. Practise walking, standing, sitting on a "throne" and speaking, in the manner of the Good King. If you try anything that doesn't work for you, or feels out of character with the Good King, simply stop and try something else. Remember, there is no failure in a rehearsal, only learning opportunities. Continue rehearsing for as long as you feel is useful.

vi) Make a few notes about how you felt, what worked and what didn't.

Unless you have been involved in a creative rehearsal process before, this exercise will feel decidedly odd at first. But if you keep working with it, it will pay dividends. It is the theatre equivalent of going to a golf range to practise some shots with a new club. You wouldn't want to try out the "new tool" for the first time in a high pressure situation, so you practise in a safe environment. In rehearsal, "failure" doesn't matter, in fact it is an essential part of the learning process. It is only by experiencing how *not* to play a character that you finally figure how you can best play it.

CUES

There are certain attributes or ways of being that are more associated with a particular character than others; "typical" ways that a character would exhibit itself in the world. There are postures, gestures, vocal tones and phrases that are more likely to come out of a Good King than out of any of the other characters. Some people find that practising these "cues" is another effective way of making the unfamiliar character more familiar. Here is a selection we have collected over the last few years:

THE GOOD KING – STATIC MASCULINE
Gives the "view from the throne".

POSTURE
Weighty, authoritative, still, upright, calm, formal.

GESTURES
Slow, methodical, balanced, solid, meaningful.

VOCAL TONE
Strong, clear, reasonable, logical, fair, dispassionate, "right", knowledgeable, authoritative.

WORDS AND PHRASES
- "Structure"
- "Objectives"
- "Points"
- "Plan"
- "Conclusions"
- "Agenda"
- "I want to advise you of..."
- "The main points to consider are..."
- "The new structure/process will be..."
- "I want to publicly acknowledge X for her contribution to..."
- "The rationale behind this is..."

Another useful technique in learning to play a less favourite character is to practise doing the things that they would do, and saying the things that they would say.

Exercise 6j: Rehearsing the Cues

You will need 10–15 minutes in a room large enough to imagine giving a presentation in. You can do this exercise by yourself, using a mirror to observe yourself, or with a colleague whose opinion you trust.

i) Look over the "cues" list above and pick one or two ideas to practise from each heading.

ii) Imagine you are about to start a presentation. Set up the room so it suits you. Now "enter" playing the Good King and begin your presentation appropriately – you only need 15–30 seconds of material.

iii) Assess your performance – how was it? Did it work? Was it believable enough for you and/or your colleague? What do you want to try differently next time?

iv) Repeat until you feel you have "claimed" the attributes you are rehearsing.

These attributes should now be more available to you in your next public presentation. You will also have a "body memory" of rehearsing the Good King to take in with you. Knowing you have done it outside the presentation room gives you an inner confidence to do it inside the next room you give a presentation in.

ACTIVITIES TO PRACTISE THE GOOD KING

And last but not least, there are certain activities that will be more associated with one character than another. The most effective long-term strategy in learning to play a less favourite character is to choose an activity associated with them and engage in it as much as your time and interest allows. Five to 10 minutes a day, or one hour a week, or a half-day every month is fine. The important thing is to pick something that you can consistently "rehearse" and that you know you can still be doing in six weeks to three months. Make it a *reasonable* time commitment, not a heavy one, or you will probably give it up before it has a chance to make a difference for you.

Good King Activities
   Action planning
   Time management
   Strategy games – chess/bridge
   Reading (non-fiction – biographies, strategy books etc)
   Reviewing
   Gathering information
   Clearing clutter
   Ordering/tidying up
   Organizing wardrobe/desk
   Listening to classical music (serious stuff like Bach).

We need to offer a small word of warning here. There is a natural temptation to take our favourite character into the environment where we can potentially learn to play our least favourite character. We worked with one advertising executive who was a natural born Medicine Woman. She identified the Good King as a "learning edge" and committed to the simple task of clearing out her wardrobe between the first programme and then report back six weeks later. On her return we asked her how it had gone. She said; "Well, I'm not sure really – I mean I started by looking through my wardrobe, but I sort of ended up redesigning the whole room." The creative side of the Medicine Woman was hard to let go of, even in the simple task of tidying up!

So, if you engage in the following exercise, remember to try and relax into the activity and let "it" inform you. If you take your favourite character to play in the new activity you will undermine the purpose.

Exercise 6k: Choosing a Good King Activity

i) Read through the list of Good King activities and choose one activity you do not currently engage in that you think will help you get to grips with Good King energy. Commit to practising it as and when your schedule allows. Make notes in your journal as to your progress and growing ease (or not) with the activity.

GOOD KING ACTION PLAN

If you have identified the Good King as a learning edge for your presentations you may already have started practising some or all of the exercises in this chapter. Wherever you have got to we would encourage you to look back through the chapter and draw up a simple action plan.

Exercise 6l: Good King Action Plan

i) Which exercises, rehearsals and/or activities are you going to practise?

ii) When and where are you going to practise?

iii) How many times?

iv) Do you have a clear goal for these practices? How will you know when you have achieved it?

v) Do you want feedback from a trusted colleague? If so, who will you ask?

The simple steps outlined in this chapter will teach you how to play the Good King better and more often. As we move through the other characters we will explore the different gifts they offer the preparation of presentations and provide similar exercises to help you learn to play them better and more often. Good luck with the rehearsals!

Chapter 7

The Great Mother – Care, Connection and The Water of Emotion

The Great Mother brings qualities of empathy, warmth, reassurance and support. One of her biggest gifts is that she is comfortable with emotion, and this helps her build caring, trusting relationships. Archetypally, emotion is linked to the element of Water. When your presentations lack emotion both you and what you are saying can seem excessively dry. In contrast, allowing an audience to feel the emotional connection you have to your material is a powerful way of increasing your impact.

This character welcomes your audience and listens to them. She knows the profound feminine power of *being with*, which is a world away from the task-focused masculine perspective. She helps you empathize with the probable emotional state of the audience before you start, and is able to "read the room" during the presentation, maintaining awareness of what is happening as the presentation progresses.

Of all the four characters, the Great Mother is often the one least played in organizational life. She doesn't compete aggressively to hit targets, and may not appear measurably productive – though she will add value to the human capital and establish a network of meaningful relationships. Here is a poem by James Autry that reveals the character's inborn "Emotional Intelligence":

THREADS

Sometimes you just connect,
like that,
no big thing maybe
but something beyond the usual business stuff.
It comes and goes quickly
so you have to pay attention,
a change in the eyes

when you ask about the family,
a pain flickering behind the statistics
about a boy and a girl in school,
or about seeing them every other Sunday.
An older guy talks about his bride,
a little affectation after twenty-five years.
A hot-eyed achiever laughs before you want him to.
Someone tells about his wife's job
or why she quit working to stay home.
An old joker needs another laugh on the way
to retirement.
A woman says she spends a lot of her salary
on an au pair
and a good one is hard to find
but worth it because there's nothing more important
than the baby.
Listen.
In every office
you hear the threads
of love and joy and fear and guilt,
the cries for celebration and reassurance,
and somehow you know that connecting those
threads
is what you are supposed to do
and business takes care of itself.

All human beings seek connection and relationship. The emergence of Emotional Intelligence as a core management competency over the last few years has been a long overdue recognition of the Great Mother gifts. In a recent interview, the great American management guru Peter Drucker named Trust as the single most important factor in determining the ability of an organization to thrive in increasingly complex times. The Great Mother embodies Trust. Here's a dramatic example of how effective this character can be in a highly charged presentation situation. It is drawn from the 1992 US election between George Bush Senior and Bill Clinton:

"The campaign reached its climax in the second presidential debate in Richmond, Virginia. The debate included spontaneous questions from the audience. The two candidates sat on high stools, were given radio mikes, and were free to wander about the stage. Toward the end of the debate, an African-American woman asked a confusing question: 'How has the national debt personally affected each of your lives? And if it hasn't, how can you honestly find a cure for the economic problems of the common people if you have no experience in what's ailing them?'

Bush: 'I'm sure it has. I love my grandchildren. I'm not sure I get… help me with the question.'

After quite a lot more such struggle, it was Clinton's turn – and he did something extraordinary. He took three steps toward the woman and asked her, 'Tell me how it's affected you again…'

The woman was speechless. Clinton helped her along, describing some of the terrible economic stories he'd heard as governor of Arkansas. But the words weren't as important as the body language. The three steps he had taken toward the woman spoke volumes about his empathy, his concern, his desire to respond to the needs of the public. Bush, by contrast, was caught gazing at his wristwatch – hoping desperately that this awkward moment would soon be past. And, indeed, it was. The presidential campaign was, in effect, over."

(From *The Natural* by Joe Klein)

Stepping into this character, even momentarily, can have a huge impact.

PART 1 – PREPARING WITH CARING

ASSESSING THE EMOTIONAL STATE OF YOUR AUDIENCE

You may have done a logical assessment of mood and the key forces affecting your audience in the Good King preparation. Assessing your audience's emotional state is a more subtle skill. Are they buoyant, depressed, anxious, angry, enthusiastic, demotivated, vulnerable, tired, excited, to name but a few? Sometimes we may need to have our antennae open to currents and signals that the Good King will not have noticed, including signals in the room itself before we start.

What is the general emotional temperature?

Starting your presentations without this awareness can lead to your audience feeling that you are not making a genuine relationship with them, particularly when there are strong emotional currents in the room. The Great Mother understands that we are all emotional creatures, whether we like it or not, and that unless our emotions are acknowledged, however briefly and implicitly, we can quickly feel alienated. Like everything else we have been talking about, this is a skill that can be developed, with practice.

Exercise 7a: Empathy

i) Next time you prepare a presentation, find a few moments when you can sit down quietly and really try and sense your audience's emotional state. If you were in their shoes what would you be feeling? What would you need to hear from a caring presenter that would make you feel acknowledged, and help you manage your emotional state?

ii) Jot down a few notes.

Was this exercise easy for you, or not? How good are you at sensing what an individual or group is feeling? Part of it is intuitive; some people just seem to "know" what others are feeling. The good news is that you can develop Emotional Intelligence.

DEVELOPING EMOTIONAL AWARENESS

For centuries, actors have had to develop the capacity to identify and convincingly portray different emotional states. What happens to people in the grip of particular emotions? One of the biggest clues lies in people's faces. We now know that several of our key facial muscles bypass the control of the frontal cortex and are directly connected to the more emotional parts of our brains. This fascinating and recent discovery means that our faces will always show some of what we are feeling, whether we like it or not! Learning to read the subtle movement of emotion in faces is a great way to develop your emotional antennae. Here is a fun way to practise:

Exercise 7b: Developing Emotional Awareness

Watch television with the sound off. It's probably best to choose a soap or drama programme. As you watch people's faces, name as many emotions as you can. As you get more practised in this, you will see that most people (and certainly most actors in a dramatic situation) are experiencing some subtle level of emotion most of the time. To help you start, below is a list of words used to describe emotional states. As you will see, there are some "prime emotions", much like primary colours in painting – Happy, Sad, Angry etc – but there are also many more subtle variations.

HAPPY	SAD	CONFIDENT	SCARED	EXCITED
Elated	Devastated	Accomplished	Fearful	Alert
Exuberant	Hopeless	Assured	Panicky	Concerned
Ecstatic	Sorrowful	Brave	Afraid	Elated
Jubilant	Depressed	Courageous	Shocked	Enthusiastic
Energized	Wounded	Determined	Overwhelmed	Highly strung
Enthusiastic	Drained	Efficient	Intimidated	Involved
Loved	Defeated	Fearless	Frantic	Stimulated
Thrilled	Exhausted	Healthy	Terrified	Aroused
Justified	Helpless	Lively	Vulnerable	Busy
Resolved	Crushed	Potent	Horrified	Delighted
Valued	Worthless	Secure	Petrified	Elevated
Gratified	Uncared for	Solid	Appalled	Exhilarated
Encouraged	Dejected	Successful	Tormented	Impatient
Optimistic	Rejected	Adequate	Tense	Curious
Joyful	Empty	Assertive	Threatened	Eager
Proud	Miserable	Capable	Uneasy	Engaged
Cheerful	Distraught	Confident	Defensive	Hyperactive
Relieved	Deserted	Dynamic	Insecure	Intrigued
Assured	Burdened	Encouraged	Sceptical	Thrilled
Determined	Demoralized	Forceful	Apprehensive	Attentive

HAPPY	SAD	CONFIDENT	SCARED	EXCITED
Grateful	Condemned	Intense	Suspicious	
Appreciated	Terrible	Self-reliant	Alarmed	
Confident	Unwanted	Strong	Shaken	
Respected	Unloved	Together	Startled	
Admired	Pitiful	Able	Guarded	
Delighted	Discarded	Bold	Stunned	
Alive	Disgraced	Competent	Awed	
Fulfilled	Disheartened	Daring	Reluctant	
Tranquil	Disappointed	Effective	Anxious	
Content	Upset	Energetic	Impatient	
Relaxed	Inadequate	Sharp	Shy	
Satisfied	Unappreciated	Sure	Nervous	
Peaceful	Discouraged		Unsure	
Hopeful	Ashamed		Timid	
Fortunate	Distressed		Concerned	
Flattered	Disillusioned		Perplexed	
Pleased	Lonely		Doubtful	
Glad	Neglected			
	Isolated			
	Alienated			

ANGRY	HELPFUL	FRUSTRATED	PLAYFUL	TIRED
Furious	Amiable	Pained	Clever	Apathetic
Seething	Compassionate	Desolate	Quick	Weak
Enraged	Cheerful	Displeased	Sharp	Absent
Hostile	Genuine	Disturbed	Funny	Listless
Vengeful	Honest	Hindered	Impish	Lethargic
Incensed	Nice	Mistreated	Bouncy	Disengaged
Abused	Optimistic	Tormented	Pesky	Beat
Humiliated	Patient	Heavy	Amusing	Done
Betrayed	Soft-hearted	Destitute	Chummy	Bushed
Rebellious	Tolerant	Dissatisfied	Frolicsome	Drained

ANGRY	HELPFUL	FRUSTRATED	PLAYFUL	TIRED
Hacked off	Appreciative	Futile	Exuberant	Worn out
Outraged	Gentle	Lost	Teasing	Empty
Spiteful	Dedicated	Abused	Mischievous	Fatigued
Resentful	Passionate	Puzzled	Humorous	Exhausted
Disgusted	Sensitive	Sore	Good-natured	Weary
Frustrated	Kind	Uneasy	Vivacious	Sleepy
Stifled	Sympathetic	Irritable	Light-hearted	Overwhelmed
Offended	Understanding	Distressed	Witty	Swamped
Displeased	Caring	Foolish	Joking	Numb
Annoyed	Comforting	Hassled	Whimsical	
Agitated	Considerate	Restless		
Irritated	Empathic	Suffering		
Exasperated	Generous	Unhappy		
Harassed	Giving			
Anguished	Involved			
Aggravated	Open			
Perturbed	Loyal			
Provoked	Sharing			
Coerced	Tender			
Cheated				
Uptight				
Dismayed				

Which of the above is closest to your emotional state, right now?

CONNECTING WITH YOUR MATERIAL

Another of the Great Mother's preparation gifts is to help you connect emotionally with your material. Once you do this there is the possibility of sharing that connection appropriately with your audience.

We coached the Chief Executive and senior staff of an international oil company. The economic climate was forcing them to make reductions in their staff. Soon, each member of the team would be travelling to different parts of the world to deliver a speech that one of our colleagues had helped them write. One part of the speech was about the cutbacks, and they had written about how sorry they were to have to do this. When they first rehearsed the delivery with us, this section was dry, and sounded like another piece of data. It had no real impact, in fact it was in danger of sounding like a platitude.

Since they were genuinely deeply sorry, particularly as some of them were going to have to lay off old friends and colleagues, it wasn't too difficult to get them to connect authentically to this feeling within themselves. They really were sad. The next step was simply to encourage them to let the feeling be present during this part of the speech. It made a huge difference. The humanity and genuine empathy they were now showing helped create a lot less alienation than might otherwise have been the case. They were human beings delivering bad news – rather than human doings delivering information. We subsequently heard that their ability to show care had made a big – and positive – difference to the impact of their presentations, and to the repercussions of their situation.

Exercise 7c: Connecting with your Material

i) From a presentation you have recently given, or from one you are about to give, choose a section that is important to you.

ii) Look through it and think about what emotional content it has, or could have.

iii) Take the time to get in touch with your real feelings about it. What do you really feel about this project/plan/pitch/idea/process etc? It may take a while to dig beneath the logic to the feelings, but stay with it. Trust whatever emerges, even if it surprises you. Remember, the Great Mother allows feelings to be there, whatever they are. In this exercise you want to discover the truthfulness of your emotions.

iv) When you get an inner sense of your emotional connection to the material, allow your awareness to expand beyond the specific presentation. What associations do you have with this feeling? Are there any other situations, private or professional, which have a similar emotional resonance for you?

v) Be with whatever arises. There is no particular outcome at this point. You are practising feeling an emotional connection. Simply acknowledge what is. Notice how it feels to allow this water to flow within you, and when you are ready, make some notes.

When it comes to delivering your presentation, you have a choice about exactly how much of these feelings you allow to be expressed. But even knowing they are there inside you is likely to impact positively on your delivery.

Of course, some feelings are more useful than others. If you are pitching a big project and are excited about it, then great! But if you are hacked off that you had to stay up all night getting it ready, watch out! Again, awareness is the key. The Great Mother can help you bring out the helpful emotional connections, and help you manage those you deem unhelpful.

MANAGING YOUR EMOTIONAL STATE

Before an important presentation almost everyone will experience some degree of nerves and anxiety. Some of this, as we have seen, is caused by the Inner Critic, but some of it is normal and inevitable. The very fact of having five, 50 or 500 people all directing their attention towards you creates pressure. The question becomes one of how to manage our emotional state in the best way. The Great Mother shows us again that the key lies in learning to accept and embrace what you are feeling, rather than pushing it away.

In Peak Performance people experience positive and buoyant emotional states. But – and this is a big BUT – we only gain access to those states *by first embracing our emotions exactly as they are.* Failing to understand this is probably the single biggest error that people make when it comes to emotion. It is a typical human response, particularly if we are feeling uptight before a presentation. Our first reaction is likely to be; "How can I stop this unhelpful feeling, how can I make it go away?" The answer is, by surrendering to it first. The water of emotion works like a wave, if we allow it to break we will be ready to feel something else – if we try and stop it then we spend all our energy maintaining a dam to try and keep it at bay.

In general, we spend a great deal of time trying to feel "good" (the emotions above the line), and a lot of energy trying to push away what we call "bad" or negative feelings (the emotions below the line).

Happy
Loving
Peaceful
Excited

Angry
Sad
Fearful
Anxious

Unfortunately, this does not work; if we deny some parts of our emotional self, we lose access to the other parts. The more we deny, the more de-energized and numb we become. In contrast, when we allow ourselves to feel our feelings just as they are, we feel more alive and Present. In fact, we can only feel the full force of those above the line if we allow ourselves to feel those below it. If we will not let ourselves feel sadness, fear, anxiety and anger, we lose access to love, happiness, peacefulness and excitement. As William Blake wrote:

> *Joy and woe are woven fine,*
> *A clothing for the soul divine.*
> *Under every grief and pine,*
> *Runs a joy with silken twine.*
> *And when this we rightly know,*
> *Safely through the world we go...*

So trying to push away "unhelpful" feelings before a presentation will leave you in an even more "unsafe" and unhelpful state. Nothing messes up our capacity to feel Present and inspired so much as unacknowledged emotion. Because you are denying a basic life force moving through you,

you will probably become more and more stiff. People will automatically feel that you are not fully "there", and this can breed mistrust.

How does this work in your experience? When you allow yourself to feel and express a strong feeling to someone close to you, and they listen to and accept your emotion, don't you feel better afterwards? More at peace with yourself, calmer?

Accepting our feelings is simple in theory, yet it can take time to learn to trust putting it into practice. Many people have an internal voice that says something like "If I don't get rid of this emotion it will overwhelm me". The Great Mother shows us that, in reality, exactly the opposite is true. The emotions you try to push away are the ones that end up controlling you, whereas once you accept an emotion within you it quickly settles and you can move on freely.

Here is an exercise to practise repeatedly, whenever you recognize that you are in an emotional state. If you are not sure whether emotion is present within you or not, try paying attention to your body. Almost every emotional state can be felt as a sensation in the body. This is reflected in our language – the "butterflies in the stomach" (anxiety), the "hairs on the back of the neck" (fear), the "lump in the throat" (sadness), "seeing red" (anger) etc. So, whenever you are feeling any kind of emotion the chances are there will be an accompanying physical sensation. In time you will learn to recognize the main patterns of your own particular repertoire of emotion/sensation.

Exercise 7d: Recognizing and Accepting Emotion

Read the instructions through first and begin when you are ready. Find yourself somewhere quiet, where you will not be disturbed for about 10 minutes.

i) Close your eyes, and take your attention inward.

ii) Notice where the strongest sensation is in your body. Take your attention there, breathe, notice this sensation as closely as you can.

iii) Ask yourself: "What is the feeling that goes with this sensation?" Name it to yourself as accurately as you can. Keep doing this. Sometimes you will find that you get drawn to another part of your body, sometimes you will

stay where you are. Just keep naming different aspects of the feeling. The key is NOT TO TRY TO CHANGE ANYTHING. Simply keep paying attention to physical sensations, and keep naming your feelings exactly as they are.
iv) You will sometimes find that when you name the feeling accurately your body will want to take a deep breath. Allow it to do so. It is an important part of you integrating the emotional energy that is running within you.
v) After a while you will probably realize that, whatever you were feeling when you started, the feeling has moved on. Usually, as you do this exercise, you will feel more and more Present, more and more settled within yourself. This is the result of you learning to name your feelings accurately to yourself.

This simple act of acknowledging your feelings allows a profound alchemy to take place. It is a key to feeling grounded, open and Present.

In this exercise you may have noticed that you had some negative reaction to some of your feelings. Perhaps some were more acceptable to you than others. Make notes about this. This is natural for most of us, particularly those for whom this character is the least favourite. We will look at some of the potential negative projections in the section on "Playing the Great Mother". First we'd like to examine her gift of awareness as you begin a presentation.

PRESENTING WITH AWARENESS

Being sensitive to the energetic and emotional state of your audience helps you to pitch your presentation appropriately from the start. While the Good King's analysis will help you prepare for what you expect to meet in the room, the Great Mother will help you adapt, in the moment, to what is actually there. To take a simple example, if you are speaking towards the end of the day – and especially if your audience has seen several presentations already – they may be tired. Whereas the Good King might simply follow his well-structured plan and play the characters he previously identified as being relevant, the Great Mother will take emerging factors into account. Her empathetic awareness may lead you to consider different, unplanned, options which might include a spontaneous change of character. For example:

1 You can – in Great Mother mode – sympathetically acknowledge your audience's fatigue right at the beginning. Often, the very act of doing this will help your audience connect with you. This in itself will change their state, helping them to feel more alert and receptive.

2 You can make sure that you start with a dynamic energy – moving into Warrior mode – and consciously reach out to your audience energetically, speaking with high energy and making lots of direct eye contact.

3 In some situations you might choose to do something playful to help them change their state – moving into Medicine Woman mode. What can you think of that might give them enough energy to hear what you need to say? Some people use humour, others take a risk and get people to do something unusual and unexpected. One of our favourites is to have people stand up, and then ask them "to interfere with the person next to you for 10 seconds". This is fun, physical and slightly risky. It always produces adrenalin and people report an immediate change of state and raised energy levels.

Throughout any or all of the above you will need to maintain Great Mother sensitivity in order to be aware of what is appropriate, when, and for how long.

When we present straight after lunch we often make reference to this being known as the "graveyard slot". Knowing that this is the time of day when the kidneys take over from the brain as the principal functioning organ is useful. Making your audience aware of this can help them choose to keep themselves alert – if you do your job properly. Acknowledging what is present in the room energetically always revitalizes a situation.

PART 2 – PLAYING THE GREAT MOTHER

Let's remind ourselves of the gifts that this character brings once you are in the presentation itself. The Great Mother:

Welcomes new people
Builds trust

Reassures in tough times
Offers support
Exudes positive feeling
Radiates warmth
Responds to concerns
Shares best practice
Is relaxed and helpful
Creates open culture
Demonstrates empathy
Is receptive
Encourages participation
Develops others.

All of these qualities emanate from a state of softness, warmth and emotional openness. Achieving them, as we saw in the chapter on "Presence", is a physical as well as a psychological process. We think of it as "taking off the armour"; showing others a bit more of who we are underneath the tough exterior. Times are changing, and our notion of what constitutes "strength" is also being redefined. Not so long ago, any sign of emotion or softness, particularly in a man, was construed as "weakness". In women it was often dismissed as "hysteria" or "unreliability". We still hear this projection in Inner Critic thoughts like "They won't respect me if I show emotion" or "Being emotional will make me look too fragile." While some organizational cultures still exhibit this outdated mindset, by and large we are coming to value a different kind of strength, one that is based on the whole person showing up.

Our friend, the poet-philosopher David Whyte, calls it "robust vulnerability". If the Good King and the Warrior give us the robustness, then the Great Mother allows us to show appropriate vulnerability. The word "appropriate" is crucial. We are not advocating an indiscriminate display of emotion. We are proposing that you allow yourself to show your passion, to acknowledge when something moves you, and to empathize with your colleagues as fellow human beings.

In theatre, the presence of contained emotion is far more powerful than either unemotional performance or uninhibited display. When there is too little water the performance is dry, when there is too much there is a risk of flooding. The former puts an audience to sleep, the latter makes them uncomfortable. But an actor has enormous impact when the audience can feel the presence of emotion in him, yet know he is in control of it. It is one of the aspects of Peak Performance that actors strive hardest to achieve. As Antony Sher said in his much-lauded book, *Year of the King*, "Real emotion is so useful. I wish I had access to it more often."

> During our two-day presentation programme, "Inspiration and Peak Performance", part of the work involves helping delegates find appropriate emotional expression. In a two-day programme with senior banking executives, all from the same organization, one delegate, Paul, was adamant: "I don't do emotion. It's not part of my work."
>
> At the end of the programme all the delegates deliver a final presentation to the group. Some choose to read a poem they have written as part of an exercise in sourcing their personal inspiration.
>
> When it was Paul's turn he took his place in front of the group and said: "I came in this morning determined not to read you my poem, but I've changed my mind." He then read a poem he had written about his two-year old son. Halfway through we all could all hear the emotion come into his voice. It was clear he was moved by the thought of his son. He contained the emotion perfectly, yet its presence was very strong. The atmosphere was electric. When he had finished, his colleagues spontaneously stood up to give him a heartfelt and sustained ovation. They had seen a softer side of him that he normally kept hidden, and it had a tremendous impact. They said that they trusted him much more and would be much more likely to follow him through difficult times.

OBSTACLES

But if the Medicine Woman is your least favourite character you may find some or all of these ideas difficult to accept. You may just have a negative opinion about this character which blocks you from acknowledging and owning the gifts. When you see someone at work for whom this is obviously a favourite character, do you appreciate them?

Or do you tend to have a few negative projections about them? Below is a typical selection we have heard over the years: over-sensitive, time-wasting, people-pleasing, pink and fluffy, intrusive, long-winded, waffling, over-emotional, deferring, procrastinating, wimpy, touchy-feely, ineffectual, self-indulgent, undisciplined and unable to hold boundaries.

Sound familiar? If so, before we explore in greater depth how to play this character, it would be useful for you to identify personal obstacles. Most Great Mother projections are underpinned by our relationship to emotion, so that is how we will focus the following enquiry.

Exercise 7e: Identifying Negative Projections about the Great Mother

This exercise will take 15–20 minutes with your journal at hand. We encourage you simply to read the questions in each numbered section and then write your answers, without thinking too much about it. Just see what comes.

i) How would you describe your relationship to emotion? How comfortable are you with your own emotions? How comfortable are you with other people's emotions? Do you trust emotion?

ii) What are your earliest memories of emotion? Did it come from parents, grandparents, other primary care givers, prefects, scout leaders, teachers, head teachers etc? Was emotional expression encouraged in your childhood? Was it a normal part of family life, or was emotion kept well zipped up?

iii) How is emotion viewed and handled in your current place of work? Is it welcomed or is it suppressed? Do you feel able to share your emotions with your colleagues and leaders? Do you think that people feel comfortable sharing their emotions with you?

iv) Shut your eyes for a few seconds and imagine a figure of a Great Mother, a figure who embodies unconditional warmth and acceptance. What do you think about them? Would you trust this imagined figure?

v) Now read over and assess your answers to the above questions. Can you see a general pattern of response emerging?

vi) If so, is it clear where this pattern of projections came from? Like many inner voices, these may have started for very good reasons. See if you can identify the causes of your current projections around emotion and the Great Mother. What in your life so far could be a cause of this pattern?

Depending on your discoveries in the above exercise you may wish to find an Inner Coach to help you, or you may decide to keep moving forwards, into Great Mother rehearsals.

EXPLORING THE GREAT MOTHER

Exercise 7f: Accessing the Great Mother

i) Close your eyes and settle yourself. Think of one person towards whom you feel great warmth, care and love. Picture them being with you right now. See where they are, how close, what they are wearing.

ii) Take some deep breaths to help you relax into the feelings you have for this person. Notice in your body how it feels to open your heart to them, and to allow the warm feelings to circulate within you.

iii) When you feel settled in this state, imagine how it would be to start talking to a group of people with this feeling of warmth and softness.

Remember how this feels, it is your entry point to the character at any time during a presentation. Going back to the first story of the chapter, it is what allowed Bill Clinton to respond so much more effectively than George Bush Senior. He was able quickly to access that caring, listening part of himself. When you embody this character, people will always feel you are personally involved and engaged with them. This is heightened when you start a sentence with the words "I feel..."

Exercise 7g: Finding Positive Images of the Great Mother

i) Personal role models – think of people that you personally know and respect, and who exhibit warm, caring energy. Make a list of them and the qualities you admire in them.

ii) Public role models – think of people in the public eye, past or present, whom you may never meet, but whom you recognize as using Great Mother qualities effectively. Some examples: Princess Diana, Mother Teresa, Oprah

Winfrey, Kofi Annan (respected as a Good King and a Great Mother), mothers/fathers with their children.

iii) Fictional role models – characters from works of fiction and/or the actors who play these parts particularly well. Madonna and child images, the Fairy Godmother in *Cinderella*, Marge Simpson, Wilma Flintstone, the Grandfather in *Heidi* etc.

Next, here is an exercise to help you find an internal image and resource. This, again, will be accessed through an Active Imagination, or a guided "waking dream".

Exercise 7h: Active Imagination to find the Great Mother

You will need 10–15 minutes undisturbed, with pen and paper, for this exercise. Read through the directions until you are familiar enough with the process to start by yourself – it is better to go all the way through the journey without stopping, if you can.

i) Close your eyes and relax. Let all your thoughts and worries disappear. Imagine with your inner eye that you can now "levitate" your body. Imagine yourself floating upwards, moving through ceilings, floors and air as necessary until you are high in the sky. Now imagine yourself flying, very fast across landscapes and over water.

ii) Now imagine that you are coming down to land in a beautiful garden. Lie down under a tree in this garden. Feel the strong, gentle presence of the tree, feel the whole place welcoming you. This is the home of the Great Mother.

iii) Now imagine her with you. Perhaps she is simply sitting beside you, perhaps she is cradling your head, perhaps she is holding you like a baby. Take whatever comes to you. Feel her unconditional love and acceptance of you.

iv) What, if anything, is she saying to you? Is there anything you want to ask her?

v) When you are ready, take your leave and retrace your steps. Imagine flying back over water and landscapes until you arrive back in the room you started from. Stretch slowly and open your eyes.

vi) As soon as you are ready, make a record of your Active Imagination journey.

Hopefully, you will by now have a few different, positive images of a Great Mother to work with. These are your resources to bring to rehearsal.

Exercise 7i: Rehearsal – Becoming the Image

This exercise will take 10–15 minutes undisturbed in a room large enough to move about in and containing a blanket on the floor.

i) Look through your notes from 7f), g) and h). Select the image of a Great Mother that you feel to be the right one to rehearse "becoming" – you can always change your mind or try a few different ones later.

ii) Lie down on the floor and practise some diaphragm breathing. Relax and let your mind empty. When you are ready, see a corridor in your mind's eye, stretching out in front of you into the distance. Imagine that there is an entrance into the corridor at the far end where someone could enter into your line of vision. Know that the Great Mother you have chosen to work with is waiting just out of your sight, at the end of the corridor.

iii) When you are ready, "allow" this Great Mother to appear at the end of the corridor and let this figure begin to move towards you. Watch the figure carefully. Examine how they walk, how they move and how they hold themselves. Allow them to keep moving towards you until they are very close; imagine them greeting you and listen to how they sound embodying their natural warmth and support.

iv) When you are ready, imagine this figure turning round and backing into your actual body, as if it were a spirit entering a physical form. Imagine how your body would feel different if this figure were actually within you. How would it change the way you think, feel, move and talk?

v) When you are ready, allow yourself to get up and stand, as if you were now the figure. Try and feel the difference between how you stand now and how you normally stand. Allow yourself imaginatively to "become" the image, and practise moving about like the figure moved in your imagination. Practise walking, standing, sitting on your blanket on the floor and speaking, in the manner of the figure you have chosen to rehearse. If you try anything that doesn't work for you, or feels out of character with the Great Mother figure you are rehearsing, simply stop, and try something else. Remember, there is no failure in a rehearsal, only learning opportunities. Continue rehearsing for as long as you feel is useful.

vi) Make a few notes about how you felt, what worked and what didn't.

The more you are able to practise and rehearse, the more comfortable you will become bringing this character into your presentation style and content.

DEVELOPING THE GREAT MOTHER

There are a number of different ways you can practise softening up and facilitating your ability to play this character. Becoming more aware of your own emotions will help you in many areas of your life. Remember that sometimes the actual feeling may be a little buried. So develop the habit of enquiring deeper into your emotional reactions. What were you really feeling in any given situation?

Exercise 7j: Great Mother Self-awareness

i) At the end of a day, look back at key events, and ask yourself what it was you were feeling at the time.

ii) Record your findings in your journal. Make this a regular practice.

Next, here are two exercises to help you practise showing more emotion, so that you can then transfer this to your presentations, and give your material emotional expression where it is appropriate.

Exercise 7k: Developing Emotional Expression

i) Find a poem or a piece of prose that moves you. Read it to yourself a couple of times and allow yourself to feel how it touches you, how it stirs emotion in you.

ii) Now read it out loud. See if you can hear the emotion in your voice, and keep going until you feel you are expressing what you feel in the piece.

iii) When you feel confident (enough) find a trusted friend or partner and read it to them. See how much of that emotion you can allow to be present in your reading. Ask them to give you feedback. Can they feel the emotion present in you? If not keep working until they can.

Exercise 7l: Practising Emotional Expression

When was the last time you expressed sadness or fear, hurt or joy to someone? With whom does it feel safe enough to do this?

i) Make an agreement with a trusted friend or colleague to have an emotionally authentic conversation on a regular basis.

ii) Talk to them about how you felt in a situation where your emotions were stirred. Try to let some of the emotion you felt in the situation be present as you talk. Explain that your goal is to become more emotionally expressive, and ask for their feedback on how much of your emotion you are allowing them to see.

If they can't feel anything as you speak, it probably means you are still talking about the feeling, as if it were data, rather than letting it be present in you as you speak. Try again.

Note: Remember, the role of your colleague or friend is not to counsel you or give advice, only to give feedback about how much of your emotion they can feel.

Time and time again we hear a presenter start by welcoming the audience, or saying how glad she/he is to be there. But how often do we feel they really mean it? Spoken with simple but genuine feeling, this kind of beginning creates a positive impact from the very start. This too, you can practise…

Exercise 7m: Beginning a Presentation

i) When you want to step into this character before a presentation, the simplest and quickest way is to think of someone you love and feel very close to. Imagine them there with you, and let your heart open to them. Feel yourself soft and warm inside. This is the core of the Great Mother feeling. (You can also call up in your imagination real and fictional figures which carry this energy for you.)

ii) Once you have settled into the core Great Mother feeling, imagine you are about to start your presentation. Picture the audience, and imagine this warm feeling extending out from the centre of your chest and embracing every single person. What will be your first few sentences of welcome? Practise saying them while staying connected to your core feeling. The words can be very simple, it's the feeling behind them that counts.

iii) When you are ready, ask a trusted colleague if you can practise this opening to a presentation with them. Ask for their feedback. How are you coming across? Can they feel your empathy and warmth?

Whatever else you may be intending with your presentation, it is often worthwhile starting off with a Great Mother welcome.

CUES

As with each of the characters, there are certain ways of being and talking that characterize the Great Mother. Some people find that practising these "cues" is an effective way of making the unfamiliar character more familiar. Below is a selection we have collected over the last few years:

THE GREAT MOTHER – STATIC FEMININE
Nurtures relationships, the audience as friend.

POSTURE
Relaxed, informal, on the same level as audience (if possible), mirroring audience.

GESTURES
Open, inclusive, friendly, supportive, responsive.

VOCAL TONE
Warm, reassuring, welcoming, positive, compassionate, heart-felt, inviting, soft, optimistic, caring.

WORDS AND PHRASES
- "Hi there…"
- "Welcome everyone…"
- "How is everyone doing today?"

- "People are our most important asset…"
- "I would like to apologize for the delay in…"
- "We wanted to create this opportunity for you to tell us…"
- "Does anyone else have a feeling that..?"
- "I know the feeling…"
- "I feel…"

Now, if you wish, you can rehearse the cues.

Exercise 7n: Rehearsing the Cues

For this exercise you will need 10-15 minutes in a room large enough to imagine giving a presentation in. You can do this exercise by yourself, using a mirror to observe yourself, or use feedback from a colleague whose opinion you trust.

i) Look over the above "cues" list and pick one or two ideas to practise from each heading.

ii) Imagine you are about to start a presentation. Set up the room so it suits the Great Mother (the less formal the better; podiums and tables can be a barrier, chairs in a semi-circle or even a complete circle is best). Now "enter" and begin your presentation using the Great Mother cues – you only need 15–30 seconds of material.

iii) Assess your performance – how was it? Did it work? Was it believable enough for you and/or your colleague? What do you want to try differently next time?

iv) Repeat until you feel you have "claimed" the attributes you are rehearsing.

These attributes should now be more available to you when you wish to call on them. You have a "body memory" of rehearsing the cues, which will give you the inner confidence to be more creative the next time you give a presentation that calls for the Great Mother.

ACTIVITIES TO PRACTISE THE GREAT MOTHER

Here is a list of suggestions that may help you develop the character of the Great Mother. Choose one of them, and make a commitment to practise it on a regular basis. Five to 10 minutes a day, or one hour a week, or a half-day each month is fine. The important thing is to pick something that you can consistently "rehearse", and that you know you will still be doing in six weeks to three months. Make the time commitment realistic or you will probably give it up before it has time to make a difference for you.

Great Mother Activities

Relaxation

Walking and being in nature

Being in or near water

Slow, hot bath with oils and candles

Gardening (though heavy digging requires Warrior energy!)

Massage, aromatherapy

Tai Chi/Yoga

Quiet time with family

Music – slow, choral, chanting.

Remember to let the new activity inform you. Be careful not to do it in the style of your favourite character or you will undermine the new learning possibility. We remember a fully signed-up Warrior who reluctantly agreed to practise adding the Great Mother to his repertoire. His only problem, he said, was that he already did all of these activities. Somewhat puzzled, we asked him if, for example, he had massages. "Oh yes indeed I do," he said, "the only thing is, I can never get them to do it hard enough, no pain, no gain!" We asked him if he spent time in nature. "Oh yes," he said, "once a month I go hawking." Finally we asked him if he spent time near water. "Absolutely," he replied, "every summer I go shark fishing." Surrender to the character you are trying to develop and you will learn from it, inflict an old style upon it and you won't.

Exercise 7o: Choosing a Great Mother Activity

Read through the above list and choose one activity you do not currently engage in that you think will help you get to grips with the Great Mother feeling. Commit to practising it as and when your schedule allows. Make notes in your journal as to your progress and growing ease (or not) with the activity.

GREAT MOTHER ACTION PLAN

If you have identified this character as your "learning edge" you may already have started practising some or all of the exercises in this chapter. Wherever you have got to we would encourage you to look back through the chapter and draw up a simple action plan.

Exercise 7p: Great Mother Action Plan

i) Which exercises, rehearsals and/or activities are you going to practise?

ii) When and where are you going to practise?

iii) How many times?

iv) Do you have a clear goal for these practices? How will you know when you have achieved it?

v) Do you want feedback from a trusted colleague? If so, who will you ask?

As you step more confidently into the Great Mother, your presentations will gain a new level of openness and warmth. People will experience you being "there" with them authentically, and their trust and respect will grow accordingly.

Chapter 8

The Medicine Woman – Imagery and Creativity

The gift that the Medicine Woman offers your presentations is access to the imagination. A picture paints a thousand words; one good image is better than "death by PowerPoint". A list of numbers we will soon forget, whereas a powerful story we can remember for years. Deep down most of us know this, but when it comes to standing and talking to groups it curiously escapes our attention.

THE POWER OF STORY

A while ago we worked with a senior police officer who had to try and motivate her close-to-retirement, and somewhat cynical, "bobbies on the beat" to engage in a new management structure with a group of new recruits. At first her presentation came across as sensible persuasion:

"You all know about the new structure we will be working with in the future, but it has come to my attention that not everyone in this borough is taking it seriously. This initiative is not going to go away, and we have got to deliver on this in order to set the benchmarking standards laid out in the Home Secretary's directive. Our new recruits are not going to be able to understand the needs of this borough unless you work closely with them on this. We will be letting down the people we are supposed to protect..."

Her colleagues – who were role-playing the bobbies in question – reported that they did not feel particularly motivated by this. They felt a bit told off and experienced her as being resentful of their position. We suggested that she try and give them a different way of thinking about the challenge in question. How could she reframe the issue in a way that did not come across as simply involving more responsibility, more paperwork and more babysitting? Could she find an image or a story that might change their perspective?

"Delivering Data"

She considered a few possibilities and then started again:

"I want to ask your help with something, but first I would like to tell you a story someone told me ages ago when I was an ambitious young bobby who thought I knew everything because I had got through basic training. The story is about a test pilot and the three things he needs to

"Telling Stories"

get home in one piece. First, of course, there are the instruments in the cockpit, which is the technology he uses to launch the plane in the right direction. Then there is the windscreen, which he uses to see where he is going. But most important of all, when he gets up in the air, is his 'seat-of-the-pants' experience, every hour he has ever spent in any plane. That's what he relies on to get him safely home. Now, you guys have that seat-of-your-pants experience. Fifteen, some of you nearly 20 years' experience on this patch. These rookies don't know anything compared to what you know about this borough. Please, help them find out. Work with them on the new structure and share your wisdom with them. Together I believe we can make this borough a safer place..."

Her colleagues spontaneously applauded her performance, the courage it had taken to tell the story, and the obviously improved result. "I'd listen to that," one said. "I saw a plane while you were talking" said another.

The human brain is built to remember pictures rather than data. As a species, human beings were telling each other stories long before they started reporting annual performance figures. We run several courses based on stories of leadership found in Shakespeare plays, partly because once you have heard a compelling story you have access to it for the rest of your life. One participant on a course wrote; "After most seminars I leave with a lever arch file packed to the gills, which becomes a doorstop three weeks later. You left me with a story I can imagine every day I need to..."

PART 1 – IMAGINING TO PREPARE

The Medicine Woman stimulates the imagination, "business speak" numbs it. One reason people give for not using images is precisely this poverty of language found in most work settings. We all know the power of the right words to change our thoughts and feelings; we remember this when we go to the theatre, see a good film or have our opinions changed by a good argument. But stand up to present to our team at work and we move into jargon. Our colleague and good friend, William Ayot, noticed this tendency early on in our work with managers and – being a poet – wrote a poem about it:

DOODLE AT THE EDGE

Another meeting, another agenda, another
list of buzz-words, initials and initiatives:
"PSU is entering Phase Three,
while the CDR wants G2 to go to Level Five."

"If we go the full nine yards on this one:
if we get pro-active, get out of the box, get
our teams together and on the same hymn-sheet;
if we hit the ground running, if we downsize HR,
if we get the money on board, and our asses into gear,
then we can change something, make a difference,
change what the other guys changed last week."

Meanwhile the god has left the garden,
the muse lies minimised in the corner of our screens.
Not dead, not buried, but ignored and unseen,
like a doodle at the edge of an action plan.

Me? I say make a sacrifice to the doodle;
pick some flowers, speak a poem, feed the tiny muse.
Draw, paint, sing or dance, and you'll bring the gods
back into the boardroom; the laughing, smiling,
weeping gods of the night-time and the wild.

You get the idea. It is not that clichés and acronyms don't have a value, it's just that they don't tend to move people from where they are to where you want them to go. They remain dry information and platitude. But any move away from "safe information" involves a risk, and here's the rub, for powerful language to land in a room full of people you have to believe in it, and you have to "see" what you are talking about. We have to find the right metaphor or image to illuminate our point.

WORKING WITH IMAGE
One of the joys of working with Shakespeare is his ability to deliver infor-

mation and impact through image. In our *Henry V* course on Inspirational Leadership we invite participants to create their own version of some of the great speeches. One of the most popular is Henry V's "Once more unto the breach" speech. He is talking to his dejected troops who have been stuck outside their first target in France for three months with no success. They had set off with a simple strategic plan; to land at Harfleur with 10,000 troops, take the town in one week, move on through France and be in Paris by Christmas. However, at the moment he delivers his famous speech, his men have been stuck outside Harfleur for three months – during which time 2,000 have died and another 3,000 are sick with dysentery. His job is to get them to go back to a small hole in the wall (the breach) they made in Week One with a bit more energy on day 91 than they had on day 90! Here's how he does it:

> *Once more unto the breach, dear friends, once more,*
> *Or close the wall up with our English dead.*
> *In peace there's nothing so becomes a man*
> *As modest stillness and humility,*
> *But when the blast of war blows in our ears,*
> *Then imitate the action of the tiger.*
> *Stiffen the sinews, conjure up the blood,*
> *Disguise fair nature with hard-favoured rage.*
> *Then lend the eye a terrible aspect,*
> *Let it pry through the portage of the head*
> *Like the brass cannon...*
> *Now set the teeth and stretch the nostril wide,*
> *Hold hard the breath, and bend up every spirit*
> *To his full height. On, on, you noblest English...*
> *Dishonour not your mothers; now attest*
> *That those whom you called fathers did beget you...*
>   *And you, good yeomen,*
> *Whose limbs were made in England, show us here*
> *The mettle of your pasture; let us swear*
> *That you are worth your breeding – which I doubt not,*

For there is none of you so mean and base
That hath not noble lustre in your eyes.
I see you stand like greyhounds in the slips,
Straining upon the start. The game's afoot.
Follow your spirit, and upon this charge
Cry, "God for Harry! England and Saint George!"

Stirring stuff. Did you see the images? Closing up the wall with English dead, imitating the action of the tiger, eyes prying through the portage of the head like a brass cannon, bending up every spirit to his full height, thinking about your mum and dad, greyhounds in the slips straining upon the start, St George. Strong images brilliantly put together to gain maximum impact. Although Henry would need access to the Warrior character to deliver this speech in a motivating way, it is the Medicine Woman who gives him access to the powerful images that move through it. Those who favour the Warrior for both preparation and delivery often do not give themselves the creative preparation time to come up with a compelling story. They focus on a few practical issues.

In our experience, most Warrior managers in Henry's position would probably say something on the lines of: "Good morning troops. Now you all know why I had to call another briefing. I did set you a very simple strategic target – 91 days ago – to take this small town of Harfleur in one week. That means that you are currently running 84 days behind schedule. This is going to have severe budget implications for the rest of the campaign, I can assure you. And that's not all; latest figures from the sick bay indicate there are now 3,000 of you claiming sick leave, while a recent communiqué from the morgue informs me there are currently 2,000 of you... dead." Which doesn't usually have quite the same effect as Henry's version!

FINDING AN IMAGE

The good news is that all of us can find images that are as effective as Henry's, when we consciously enter the realm of the Medicine Woman. And, what is even better news for most of us, is that we don't have to do it in iambic pentameter! It helps if we can find a way to reframe the problem as an *opportunity,* and look for a positive picture to change the perception of others. A business parable tells of a European shoe manufacturer who sent two marketing managers to a remote region of Africa to assess expansion possibilities. The first sends an e-mail saying: "Situation hopeless – no-one here ever wears shoes." The second reports: "Fabulous opportunity, they have no shoes!" Which message do you think you would be more likely to send?

> We were coaching Paul, an IT manager whose project was getting stuck. Everyone was working late pretty much every day, and all they seemed to be doing was uncovering more problems with the new system. He wanted to help them move through the blocks, but mostly what he had on his mind was the pressure he was under to deliver. This was how he started off in his first coaching session:
>
> "OK guys, I know you're tired, but we just can't stop. You know the front office have decided on the due date and we are coming up to it pretty fast. I think it's fair to say that all our reputations are on the line here, and we have got to come up with more solutions quicker than we are currently doing. I have had over 15 complaints delivered to me in the past week alone..."
>
> At which point, seeing the expressions on the role-players' faces, we stopped him: "It sounds like you're telling them 2,000 of them are dead!" we said. He got the point. We asked him to think of things outside of work that he had a personal interest in and select one that he was passionate about. He said running marathons. So now we asked him to relate his current work situation to running a marathon, with the proviso that he give a positive rather than a negative message to his overworked staff. We asked him to remember some dramatic images from marathons he had run and see which one might best fit his current situation. When he felt ready we asked him to close his eyes for a brief moment and really take himself back to the moment he was going to talk about. Then he started again:
>
> "Listen up guys, we're in this for the long haul and we are going to make it. I was just thinking about running the London Marathon last year. It started great – everyone excited and raring to go – the first 10 miles were

pretty good. Then I started noticing everyone around me; instead of being comrades in arms they started annoying me, you know 'Why can't he keep out of my way, can't he see that's where I want to go?' Another five miles and my legs started to get heavy, I started doubting myself: 'God, am I really going to finish, how embarrassing it would be to pull out now, what would everyone say?' By the time I got to 21 miles I hit 'the wall' – the bit in me that was ready to give up. I was on the point of stopping when someone beside me shouted 'Come on guys, let's keep going, only five miles to go!' 'God,' I thought, 'if I stop now I'll never know the joy of finishing, I don't want to miss that, think how good you'll feel crossing the finish line – see the line – see yourself crossing it. I can do it, I've done it before and I'll do it again – this is not the time to quit, it's the time to dig deep and make it happen.' And I did. And it did feel great to finish. Can you guess why I thought of that now? Yup, we're at the 21-mile mark. We've hit the wall on this project – big time – so it's time to dig deep and help each other finish. Think how good we're going to feel when we get to our finishing line. It's going to be worth it. "

He looked around at the big smiles on the faces of his audience. The message had been received loud and clear and had created positive energy in the room.

So now it's your turn. Remember that if the Medicine Woman is a less favourite character of yours then the following exercises may be difficult; we recommend that you practise a few times until they become more familiar. If, however, the Medicine Woman is a favourite character of yours, chances are that you do a lot of what we have been talking about already – whether consciously or unconsciously. We recommend that you at least read through the exercises to see if there is anything you might like to try.

Exercise 8a: Finding an Image

You will need 10–15 minutes for this exercise, with journal and pen.
i) Think of a current situation that appears stuck or that is getting others down.

ii) Write down the logical facts and data about the situation.

iii) Now get creative with it, think around the issue; what else can you imagine that this situation is like? Try to find a few different images, stories and/or metaphors from different arenas – maybe one from a favourite hobby or activity of yours, one from sport, one from nature and one from fiction (book, cartoon, soap opera or movie). Or anything else that takes your fancy – the Medicine Woman tends to make it up as she goes along.

iv) Now pick the image, metaphor or story that grabs you the most – the one that inspires you.

v) Find a way of relating the image to the situation. How can you link the two together in a way that might change others' perception about the situation? It might take a while or a few goes, or it might come quickly and easily. The ways of the Medicine Woman are mysterious, you can't plan it, but you will usually know when you find it.

vi) When you are ready, find a colleague you can test it out with: "If I were to use this image when talking about that situation would it be helpful..?" And rehearse it with them. Did it help them to understand the situation in a different way? Was it helpful? If so, you've found yourself a good image, if not, try again until you do...

The root of the word "image" is the same root as the word "magic" and that of "magi" (as in the Three Wise Men). The real magic of an image is that when we imagine a picture it can actually change how we feel and the sensations we experience in our body. Try looking at a favourite photo of a loved one, and you'll probably feel what we mean. If we talk about an image that means something to us we can instil that image in the minds of others in such a way that they will remember it.

METAPHORICAL THINKING
Those of us for whom the Medicine Woman is the least favourite character are likely to be entertaining one or two of those "inner voices" around thinking metaphorically. If you become aware of them note them down. If they really get in your way you may need a return trip to the Inner Coach. If they are manageable, see if what follows can help.

Images are everywhere. We are being informed by them all the time, every day – whether we are conscious of it or not. So if you find it difficult to access the imagination on demand and come up with your own images, then beg, borrow or steal them. Shakespeare did not invent a single main plot in all his plays, he borrowed them from history and stole them from other storytellers and playwrights. It worked for him! The following are two exercises that will help you work with images and develop metaphorical thinking.

Exercise 8b: Borrowing an Image to Create a Metaphor

If you find it hard to come up with your own images, stories and metaphors the solution is simple – borrow them.

i) Think about where you could find some useful images. You might go to a poster store or an art gallery; you might buy some photographic or graphic magazines, or click onto an image store website.

ii) Look at a group of pictures and think about which ones suit you today. They may have a resonance with a personal mood or a current working reality. What is it about them that fits? Let your imagination guide you in making unusual connections.

iii) Write about it in your journal or describe it to a trusted friend.

Now for an example from business:

We were coaching John, an HR manager who had a block around working with images. We sent him home after his first coaching session to find some images he could relate to his current working reality. He was an enthusiastic traveller and remembered that he had a box full of old copies of *National Geographic* magazine stored in his attic. He committed to looking through them before his next session. When he came back he showed us pictures of the Himalayas featuring some nomads with donkeys moving uphill in the far distance. "I felt a resonance with this picture. I feel my work is all uphill at the moment and I am struggling to get to a peak where I can set up camp and get some perspective." Simple and effective – John was using a borrowed image to stimulate his metaphorical thinking.

Exercise 8c: Problem Solving with Images

i) Think of a current problem or issue.

ii) Now imagine it as a picture (try not to think too hard) and draw what you see. Draw an image that represents the problem, with no words. How literal is it? If your attempt to draw an overspent budget involves a £ or $ sign and a minus, it's still pretty literal!

iii) Now (if you haven't already) find an image from nature that can express (near enough) the same thing. That should move it more to the metaphorical level.

iv) Now look at the metaphorical image of the original problem. What needs to happen to the image to "solve" the metaphorical problem and/or make it better?

v) Draw a new picture which resolves the metaphorical problem expressed in the first image. Be intuitive, don't think too hard.

vi) Now, think how you could translate the second picture image into a working reality. If you could solve the problem via the image – what needs to happen in real life to get the same kind of improved result? Be open-minded, allow a few crazy ideas to come in, don't judge them too soon.

Consider an excerpt from one of the most famous dreams of the last century, a speech given by the Civil Rights leader Martin Luther King:

> "I have a dream that one day on the red hills of Georgia the sons of former slaves and the sons of former slave owners will be able to sit down together at the table of brotherhood.
>
> I have a dream that one day even the state of Mississippi, sweltering with the heat of injustice and oppression, will be transformed into an oasis of freedom and justice.
>
> I have a dream that my four little children will one day live in a nation where they will not be judged by the colour of their skin but by the content of their character. I have a dream today."

He took a real problem – racism – and found a powerful metaphor to represent the problem – "a state, sweltering with the heat of injustice and oppression". But before he gives us the answer to the real, political problem, he gives us the solution to the metaphorical problem; "an oasis of freedom and justice". Once his audience "saw" these two powerful images they would be compelled to listen to his "real-time solution" that would turn the desert into the oasis. It has remained one of the most powerful speeches in history.

The images sell the message and make it memorable and compelling. Did Martin Luther King say; "I have a strategic plan"? He did not. Of course, he needed a strategic plan to implement the dream – but the dream came first. The images he used were easily memorable and continued to inspire those he was speaking to during the long process of making the dream a reality.

EFFICIENCY VS EFFECTIVENESS

Arthur C Clarke once wrote; "For every problem there is a solution that is simple, logical and wrong!" We often feel safer being logical and efficient at work and in presentations. But true effectiveness combines appropriate logic with creative thinking and passion.

When we allow the pressure to deliver targets to numb our creative minds and eradicate images we end up with a dry, turgid working environment. The right imagery can add meaning to our work. When we allow the pressures around us to limit our imaginations we lose something important. Consider the following, given to me by an assistant chief executive of a local council:

Last year, in the middle of an intense efficiency drive, the Chief Executive was invited to a local charity concert. He did not have time to go but asked the Management Services Officer, in charge of the efficiency drive, to go in his place. Being a good employee he sent a report to the Chief Executive of his experience at the concert. The concert was Schubert's unfinished Symphony. These were his views:
1 For considerable periods the four oboe players had nothing to do. Now their numbers should be reduced and their work spread over the whole orchestra, thus eliminating peaks of inactivity.

2 All of the 12 violins were playing identical notes. Now this seems an unnecessary duplication and the staff in this section should be cut drastically. If a larger sound is really required this could be obtained through electronic amplification.

3 Much effort was absorbed in the playing of demi, semi-quavers. Now this seems an excessive refinement and it is recommended that all the notes should be rounded up to the nearest semi-quaver. If this were done it will be possible to use trainees and lower graded operators.

4 No useful purpose is served by repeating with the horns the same passage that has already been played by the strings. If all such redundant passages were eliminated the concert could be reduced from two hours to 20 minutes. If Schubert had attended to these matters he would probably have had time to finish the bloody thing.

(Adapted from the satirist, Hoffnung)

The use of appropriate imagery may not seem efficient, but it will be effective.

PART 2 – PLAYING THE MEDICINE WOMAN

Let's remind ourselves of the presentation gifts of this character. She or he:

Imagines the future
Creates vision
Paints pictures
Uses metaphor
Dares to dream
Is enthusiastic
Animates others
Inspires the new
Creates change
Excites possibilities
Brainstorms
Encourages adaptability
Sparks "out of the box" thinking.

The Medicine Woman knows how to take people on a vivid imaginative journey, even if briefly. She helps people to think "out of the box" and see new possibilities. Sometimes she uses creative means to do so, such as using props, physically enacting a story as she tells it or reading a poem. She helps people dare to dream. She speaks enthusiastically and has the ability to respond spontaneously to the situation during a presentation, taking the risk of improvising her words and actions. At best, her creative energy is exciting and inspiring. However dry your presentation may be, injecting one short passage of Medicine Woman energy – such as an image or a story – may be the thing that transforms its impact.

SEEING THE IMAGE

The key to delivering an image to its full effect during a presentation is that you yourself must "see" it as you speak it. If you simply talk about an image it becomes another piece of information, and fails to engage the audience's imagination. When you allow yourself to see it vividly, there is a high probability that your listeners will see it too. Once you achieve this, you will have engaged them powerfully.

Exercise 8d: Seeing the Image

i) Take an image, story or metaphor – the one from 8a) is fine.

ii) Close your eyes and concentrate on making that image, story or metaphor Present for yourself. Immerse yourself in it. See it. Now imagine talking about it, keeping the image as visible and Present for yourself as you can.

iii) If possible, practise this with a friend or colleague. Ask them for feedback as to whether a) they felt you were seeing the image, and b) whether they also saw the image you were describing.

iv) The next time you try and work with an image during an actual presentation, take a moment before you start to summon up the image, story or metaphor in your mind's eye. Really try and draw on your image during the presentation. If you see it clearly, so should your audience.

USING PROPS

The creative use of props can add greatly to the impact of your message. The right object, used at the right time, will make your message more vivid.

A law firm was engaged in a major change initiative, which included the installation of a new online research facility. There had been a lot of grumbling and resistance, not least because of the 100-year tradition of researching in dusty, leather-bound tomes in the library. One day the CEO called a partner meeting and stood on the stage lit by a single shaft of light. "We have come here today to talk about the future," (a light went up stage left on a shiny laptop) "but before we do that I would like us to honour the past" (a light went up stage right on a pile of old, leather-bound tomes). "These law books have been the heart and soul of our work for over a hundred years. Collectively, we as a firm have spent literally years working with them, but all good things come to an end" (a junior clerk entered stage right and picked up the books). "Would you please join me in acknowledging the past." He started clapping, applauding the books as they were slowly walked offstage. The partners joined in, clapping for several minutes. When they were finished, the spotlight stage right faded to black. Now the partners were ready to hear about the future.

Exercise 8e: Using Props

i) Find a recent presentation. Think through the main points.

ii) Pick a point that you could make physical in some way. Imagine a prop you could use to make the point more vividly.

iii) Find the relevant prop and practise by yourself, using it to make the point with more impact.

iv) Find a colleague you can try it out on and get their feedback.

OBSTACLES

If the Medicine Woman is one of your less favourite characters, you might find some or all of her gifts difficult to access in your presentations.

As a young up-and-coming actor, Richard's father, Laurence Olivier, was cast in the role of Sergei, a self-obsessed soldier in the George Bernard Shaw play *Arms and the Man*, directed by Tyrone Guthrie. A couple of weeks into rehearsal Tyrone took him aside to say that his performance was not working, primarily because it was obvious that Laurence did not enjoy playing the character. Laurence replied; "But he's such an arrogant bastard, how could I enjoy playing him?" To which Tyrone responded; "You must learn to love him. Until you do, you will never be able to play him properly."

When you see someone at work for whom the Medicine Woman is obviously a favourite character, do you recognize and appreciate their gifts? Or do you tend to have negative projections about them? Remember, these projections are the obstacles to you inhabiting (and "loving") the character. Some popular negative projections about Medicine Women are that they are: unrealistic, mad, chaotic, inconsistent, ridiculous, fanciful, ungrounded, off on a tangent, pie in the sky, arty-farty, unprepared, time-wasting, always reinventing the wheel, unfocused on results, easily distracted, creating change for change's sake, dreamers and/or "only interested in their own ideas".

Of course, there are some addicted Medicine Women around who do manifest these behaviours, but if you project the negative onto Medicine Women before you see their gifts you will find it difficult to access those gifts in your presentations.

We were working with a top team in Portugal. They had to negotiate a change in direction for the company against internal resistance, and sell their ideas for the future in a compelling way. As they worked on the coast, in full view of the ocean, they decided to use the image of a boat, pulling down sails and putting up different ones to ride out a storm. However, when the MD, Phillippe, came to rehearse presenting this image it had no life. He was stiff and formal and it wasn't working. He identified that his favourite character was the Good King, and his least favourite the Medicine Woman. He reported a inner voice saying "Be sensible, don't make a fool of yourself." We asked him to trace the potential origins of this voice and he remembered a time early in his career as a junior accountant. He had been sitting in on an annual report meeting where a more senior and very flamboyant colleague had started telling inappropriate jokes. They had not gone down well and his firm had ended up losing a big client.

We did an Inner Coach exercise and helped Phillippe find a Coach who validated his right to be creative and expressive. We led him through some Active Imaginations to gain access to positive images of the Medicine Woman – which included his favourite artist Salvador Dali, a real creative maverick. We then gave him a few more in-depth rehearsals where we encouraged him to imagine he was in a storm while he was talking about the image. By the time we had finished he was telling a compelling story that was engaging every member of his top team.

So, before we suggest exercises to help you play the Medicine Woman, it would be helpful for you to think what obstacles might get in your way.

Exercise 8f: Identifying Negative Projections about the Medicine Woman

This exercise will take 10–15 minutes with your journal at hand. We encourage you simply to read the questions in each numbered section and then write your answers, without thinking too much about it. Just see what comes.

i) How would you describe your relationship to creativity? How do you generally regard people who express themselves freely and spontaneously? Do you generally trust creative people? If not, what is it that you usually think about them when you are in their presence and/or on the receiving end of their latest dreams and ideas? Write without censoring yourself. Names, words, phrases, anything that comes to mind.

ii) What were your earliest memories of creativity? Was creativity exhibited by parents, grandparents, other primary care givers, prefects, scout leaders, art and dance teachers, head teachers..? Was creativity encouraged in your childhood? Did you admire people who thought "outside the box" or were you more likely to think of them as unruly rebels?

iii) How is creativity viewed in your current place of work? Is it genuinely encouraged or does a logical approach tend to win the day? Do you feel able to take your creative ideas to senior managers and leaders? Do you think that your people feel comfortable sharing their creative ideas with you?

iv) Shut your eyes for a few seconds and imagine a figure of a Medicine Woman or Magician. What do you think about them? Would you trust this imagined figure?

v) Now read over and assess your answers to the above questions. Can you see a general pattern of response emerging?

vi) If so, is it clear where this pattern of projections came from? Like many inner voices, these may have started for excellent reasons. See if you can identify the causes of your current projections around creativity and the Medicine Woman. What in your life so far could be a cause of this pattern?

If you have found a strong critical voice you may wish to consider revisiting "The Inner Coach" chapter with it, to find an antidote. If it feels manageable enough as it is, then try some of the rehearsal suggestions below. We will start by finding positive images of the Medicine Woman in personal and public life, in history and fiction to build a positive pool of reference.

Exercise 8g: Finding Positive Images of the Medicine Woman

i) Personal role models – think of people that you personally know and respect, and who exhibit spontaneous creative energy. Make a list of them and the qualities you admire in them.

ii) Public role models – think of people in the public eye (past or present) whom you may never meet, but whom you recognize as using Medicine Woman energy effectively. Some popular names in seminars have been: Anita Roddick, JK Rowling, Princess Diana, The Dalai Lama, Richard Branson, Robin Williams, Paul McKenna, Jane Austen, Michelangelo, Salvador Dali.

iii) Fictional role models – characters from works of fiction and/or the actors who play these parts particularly well. Merlin, Serena "the teenage witch", Phoebe (character from *Friends*), Harry Potter, Dr Dolittle, Obi-Wan Kenobi, Lieutenant Columbo.

You will need to appreciate the gifts of the Medicine Woman before you will be able to play her effectively in presentations. If you can't find any positive images you may yet need to revisit the "Inner Coach" exercise to gain some inner support for this process. If you have some external images and resources you should be ready to find an internal image and resource. This will be accessed through Active Imagination.

Exercise 8h: Active Imagination to Find the Medicine Woman

You will need 10–15 minutes undisturbed, with pen and paper. Read through the directions until you are familiar enough with the process to start by yourself; it is better to go all the way through the journey without stopping, if you can.

i) Close your eyes and relax. Let all your thoughts and worries disappear. Imagine with your inner eye that you can now "levitate" your body. Imagine yourself floating upwards, moving through ceilings, floors and air as necessary until you are high in the sky. Now imagine yourself flying, very fast, across landscapes and over water.

ii) Now imagine a forested landscape coming closer. Move towards it and land in a clearing in the forest. Know that there is a hut nearby, with a Medicine Woman inside, waiting to meet you. Imagine finding your way to the hut and meeting the Medicine Woman. Have a brief interaction; observe her carefully – how she acts, talks, plays, engages with the world and with you.

iii) When you are ready, take your leave and retrace your steps. Imagine flying back over water and landscapes until you arrive back in the room you started from. Stretch slowly and open your eyes.

iv) As soon as you are ready, write a record of your Active Imagination journey.

Note: In these Active Imaginations to find the characters we will invite you to imagine the archetypal gender associated with the character. If you find this difficult or uncomfortable you are welcome to change the gender, from Medicine Woman to Magician.

Hopefully, by now you will have a few different, positive images of a

Medicine Woman to work with. These are your resources to bring to rehearsal.

Exercise 8i: Rehearsal – Becoming the Image

This exercise will take 10–15 minutes undisturbed, in a room large enough to move about in and containing a blanket on the floor.

i) Look through your notes from 8g) and h). Select the image of a Medicine Woman that you feel to be the right one to rehearse "becoming" – you can always change your mind or try a few different ones later.

ii) Lie down on the floor and practise some diaphragm breathing. Relax and let your mind empty. When you are ready, see a corridor in your mind's eye, stretching out in front of you into the distance. Imagine that there is an entrance into the corridor at the far end where someone could enter into your line of vision. Know that the Medicine Woman you have chosen to work with is waiting just out of your sight, at the end of the corridor.

iii) When you are ready, "allow" this Medicine Woman to appear at the end of the corridor and let this figure begin to move towards you. Watch the figure carefully. Examine how they walk, how they move and how they hold themselves. Allow them to keep moving towards you until they are very close, imagine them greeting you and listen to how they sound embodying their natural magic and creativity.

iv) When you are ready, imagine this figure turning round and backing into your actual body, as if it were a spirit entering a physical form. Imagine how your body would feel different if this figure were actually within you. How would it change the way you think, feel, move and talk?

v) When you are ready, allow yourself to get up and stand, as if you were now the figure. Try and feel the difference between how you stand now and how you normally stand. Allow yourself imaginatively to "become" the image, and practise moving about like the figure moved in your imagination. Practise walking, standing, sitting on your blanket on the floor and speaking, in the manner of the figure you have chosen to rehearse. If you try anything that doesn't work for you, or feels out of character with the Medicine Woman figure you are rehearsing, simply stop and try something else. There is no failure in a rehearsal, only learning opportunities. Continue rehearsing for as long as you feel is useful.

vi) Make a few notes about how you felt, what worked and what didn't.

The more you are able to practise and rehearse, the more comfortable you will become bringing this character into your presentation style and content.

CUES

There are certain attributes or ways of being that are typically associated with the Medicine Woman. Practising these "cues" is another effective way of making the unfamiliar character more familiar. Below is a selection we have collected over the last few years:

THE MEDICINE WOMAN – DYNAMIC FEMININE
Conjures a new perspective.

POSTURE
Light, airy, informal, breezy.

GESTURES
Varied, open, unpredictable, spontaneous, mirroring, uses appropriate body language to provoke new thought.

VOCAL TONE
Variable, questioning, animated, excited, bright, musical, evocative – no set pattern, unstructured – pictures form as thoughts crystallize that emerge in the room, in the moment!

WORDS AND PHRASES
- "Imagine"
- "Create"
- "Picture this…"
- "Metamorphosis"
- "Experiment"
- "I sense this is happening"
- "Vision"

- "What if..?"
- "Symbols and metaphors – what does this mean?"
- "What do you make of this?"
- "New ways – rip up the template"
- "Have some fun!"

Now, if you wish, you can rehearse the cues.

Exercise 8j: Rehearsing the Cues

You will need 10–15 minutes in a room large enough to imagine giving a presentation in. You can do this exercise by yourself, using a mirror to observe yourself, or incorporate feedback from a colleague whose opinion you trust.

i) Look over the above "cues" list and pick one or two ideas to practise from each heading.

ii) Imagine that you are about to start a presentation. Set up the room so it suits the Medicine Woman (the less formal the better, podiums and tables can be a barrier). Now "enter" and begin your presentation using the Medicine Woman cues – you only need 15–30 seconds of material.

iii) Assess your performance – how was it? Did it work? Was it believable enough for you and/or your colleague? What do you want to try differently next time?

iv) Repeat until you feel you have "claimed" the attributes you are rehearsing.

These attributes should now be more available to you when you wish to call on them. You have a "body memory" of rehearsing the cues, which will give you the inner confidence to be more creative the next time you give a presentation which calls for the Medicine Woman.

ACTIVITIES TO PRACTISE THE MEDICINE WOMAN

The most effective long-term strategy in learning to play a less favourite character is to choose an activity associated with them and engage in it as much as your time and interest allows. Some 5–10 minutes a day, or one hour a week, or a half-day every month is fine. The important thing is to pick something that you can consistently "rehearse" and that you know you can still be doing in six weeks to three months. Make it a reasonable time commitment not a heavy one, or you will probably give it up before it has time to make a difference for you.

Medicine Woman Activities

Almost anything artistic or creative:
   Painting
   Singing
   Dancing
   Writing and reading poetry and/or fiction
   Pottery and/or sculpture
   Amateur dramatics
   Playing made-up games with children
   Self-expression workshops
   Spontaneity – doing unplanned things on the spur of the moment
   Doing the unfamiliar – even finding a new route to work will help
   Practise brainstorming and/or creative problem solving
   Playing a musical instrument
   Listening to and/or playing jazz music.

Remember to let the new activity inform you. If you are not careful, your favourite character might just show up at the wrong time and undermine the learning opportunity. We fondly remember a Good King accountant who determined to practise the Medicine Woman by going to an expressive dance class once a week for three months, only to end up becoming the dance teacher's financial advisor, with no time to dance!

Exercise 8k: Choosing a Medicine Woman Activity

i) Read through the above list of Medicine Woman activities and choose one activity you do not currently engage in that you think will help you get to grips with the Medicine Woman energy. Commit to practising it as and when your schedule permits. Make notes in your journal as to your progress and growing ease (or not) with the activity.

MEDICINE WOMAN ACTION PLAN

If you have identified this character as your "learning edge" you may already have started practising some or all of the exercises in this chapter. Wherever you have got to, we would encourage you to look back through the chapter and draw up a simple action plan.

Exercise 8l: Medicine Woman Action Plan

i) Which exercises, rehearsals and/or activities are you going to practise?

ii) When and where are you going to practise?

iii) How many times?

iv) Do you have a clear goal for these practices? How will you know when you have achieved it?

v) Do you want feedback from a trusted colleague? If so, who will you ask?

We will leave you with a little poetic inspiration for your rehearsals, some of the joy and inspiration that the Medicine Woman offers you at work:

THE IDEA

Even the coffee tastes good today.
Hunched over tables, leaning in,
excitement building in a rising circle –
excited looks, excited gestures,
grunts of approval, exclamations,
"*That's it... Like that... Mmm... Exactly*
We've been working on that one too..."
Laughter now, layered with delight,
connection colliding with coincidence,
synapses snapping to amazed attention,
everything informing the one idea.

And somewhere out there, a shapeless notion,
waiting to be noticed, to be landed, pulled in –
the missing piece, the vital ingredient,

the essential component, Factor X.

In its own time it comes, arising naturally,
named just the once or merely inferred,
gathering itself with implosive momentum,
like demolition footage run in reverse:
a cloud of rubble unsettling itself,
bricks flying in from all directions,
forming, rising out of dusty chaos,
towering, complete and wholly new.

Then, the silence, the precious moment,
the circle of sparkling, enlivened eyes,
the unspoken praise in every smile,
the collective sigh that says, This is it.

(William Ayot)

Chapter 9

The Warrior – Action and Commitment

The Warrior embodies drive, commitment and focus. He asserts his point of view strongly, motivates confidently and issues a call to action. He helps others achieve great results, and is not afraid to challenge poor standards and behaviour. Whatever the goal or target, he will achieve it. The shape we ascribe to the Warrior is an arrow. He knows where he is going and what he wants.

We see a lot of Warrior behaviour in organizational life, but of all the four characters he is the one whom we probably most see in the negative form – bullying, domineering and aggressive. This can lead some people, particularly those who favour the Great Mother, to think that he has nothing positive to offer. This is a huge loss. Although we often associate the Warrior with battle, it is his inner qualities that count, not the literalness of fighting. Without the Warrior very little gets done. The Medicine Woman may have great ideas, and the Great Mother will support and nurture people, but it is the Warrior who gets out there in the front line, rallies the troops and puts the plans into action.

The Warrior is disciplined. For example, once he has identified a physical regime that will serve him he sticks to it rigorously. "I don't feel like it today" is entertained for a couple of seconds then dismissed! He sets himself demanding targets, and sticks to them. This is the person who goes to the gym and pushes through the pain barrier each time to do more sit-ups, more bench presses. This is the person who decides to compete in a marathon and then puts themselves through a challenging training routine during the winter months. However often they might feel like calling the whole thing off, their sense of commitment and purpose carries them through. If you think of any people you know or hear of who have stuck with a project – personal, sporting or professional – seeing it through all kinds of difficulties and barriers, these people will have had access to Warrior energy.

PART 1 – THE WARRIOR PREPARES

The Warrior offers several gifts. First, he does as much preparation as is necessary, persevering through fatigue barriers if need be, until he is satisfied.

Secondly, he is willing to take risks with the content. He will sell his vision with passion, fire people up with his conviction and challenge others as and when necessary.

Exercise 9a: Taking a Risk

You will need an old or upcoming presentation to work with.

i) Read through it and ask yourself how safe you felt you were/are being with the material and how you frame it.

ii) Try and identify one place where you could take more of a risk, be more assertive, speak with more conviction or issue a challenge. Write or practise speaking while incorporating this risk.

iii) If you feel ready, find a trusted colleague willing to hear your "risk", and get feedback from them. If you don't feel ready yet, practise some of the other exercises in this chapter until you do.

Thirdly, the Warrior makes sure that everything he wants and needs for his presentation is in place; the technology, the lights, the props and the room layout. If he arrives at a venue and sees that the chairs would be better in a different layout or direction, he gets it changed, even if it makes him unpopular. And even if he does it himself, at midnight!

Exercise 9b: Getting it Right

The next time you give a presentation, check out the room in advance.

i) Stand in the space and make sure everything is in the right place for you. How could you make it better?

ii) Be assertive. Get it changed. Notice how comfortable (or not) you feel as you do this.

PART 2 – PLAYING THE WARRIOR

Let's sum up his presentation gifts. The Warrior:

Sells vision
Motivates others
Instils belief
Confronts complacency
Focuses on results
Encourages competition
Rouses passion
Uses forceful persuasion
Exudes confidence
Sets tough targets
Gives a "call to arms"
Exudes will-power
Is inspiring
Challenges people to win.

During a presentation the Warrior brings in a fiery, dynamic energy evident in his voice, his language, his gestures and his overall physical presence. He leaves you in no doubt as to what his goals are, and at best his energy is highly infectious.

OBSTACLES

Just as with the other characters, it is often our negative opinion about a least favourite character that is the prime obstacle to accessing their valuable gifts. When you see someone at work obviously enjoying the Warrior do you appreciate it, or do some of those negative projections creep in? Popular projections about the Warrior include that he is: a bully, intimidating, dominating, aggressive, impatient, blaming, heavy-handed, driven to win at all costs, blood thirsty, out for himself, always in a hurry, inconsiderate and uncaring.

Of course, there are people who are negative, addicted Warriors. When these people are not connected to a purpose beyond themselves they can be destructive. When we see this bullying behaviour in others we start worrying about stepping into the character. The Inner Critic says, "They'll think I'm a bully" or "They'll think I don't care about them any more" or "They won't like me if I am that determined."

However, if we can see and recognize this behaviour in others, it means we are aware of it, and will be able to pull back from going too far. Your job is to learn to go into it sufficiently to access the gifts.

Personal obstacles to playing the Warrior often manifest as a lack of self-confident assertiveness. This may have its origins in the past. If experience has taught us that our assertiveness is unwelcome we may cut it out of our repertoire and then find it difficult to call it back when we need it.

Lin was a senior HR manager in a large bank. She often had to give presentations whose goal was to sell a new training initiative to reluctant managers. She recognized that she really needed more Warrior energy to achieve this. When we role-played this, and she came in to try to sell us a programme, her energy was very flat. No Warrior at all. We talked about the kind of fire and assertiveness she needed. When asked if she could recall ever being able to access that kind of energy she immediately recounted the following scenario: she had a bullying elder brother who used to take her toys away from her whenever he felt like it. This made her really angry, but whenever she started to express this anger her parents immediately stopped her. They took her brother's side, and told her that girls shouldn't express themselves in a loud, angry way, and she should learn to control herself. This had happened time and time again. It was hardly surprising that she couldn't assert herself strongly now.

Following the kind of procedure we described in "The Inner Coach" chapter, we began by role-playing the original situation as it occurred. She saw her brother taking her toys, she felt her anger, and then her two parents stopped her expressing it. She experienced all the frustration this caused her.

Then we created the antidote. We brought in two imaginary parents, "the parents she could have had back then". We re-started the scene, and at the moment when she started to get angry her "new" parents gave her some different messages. "We fully support you in your anger. We love it when you assert yourself like that. You have every right to be angry with him." She felt tremendously supported by these statements.

When she had taken in this antidote to her satisfaction we returned to her original presentation. This time she came in and spoke with fierce passion and conviction. The transformation was quite breath-taking. Her audience applauded strongly and told her they would be much more ikely to buy her training initiative now she was selling it with Warrior energy.

If this is a less favourite character for you, it will be valuable for you to identify your negative projections about the Warrior before you try and play him.

Exercise 9c: Identifying Negative Projections about the Warrior

This exercise will take 15–20 minutes with your journal at hand. We encourage you simply to read the questions in each numbered section and then write your answers, without thinking too much about it. Just see what comes.

i) How would you describe your relationship to assertiveness and fearlessness? How comfortable are you with these qualities, in yourself and in others? (Assertiveness is about being open, honest and direct. It is about asking for what you want or need, while recognizing that others also have needs. It should not be confused with aggressive or appeasing behaviour.)

ii) Do you generally trust people who play the Warrior? If not, what do you usually think when you come into contact with them? Write down words, phrases – anything that comes to mind.

iii) What are your earliest memories of Warrior energy? Parents, grandparents, other primary care givers, teachers, head teachers etc – did they encourage this in you?

iv) In general terms, as a child, was your enthusiasm and physical energy appreciated? Were you ever told, or made to feel, it was too much?

v) How is drive and ambition viewed in your current place of work and/or in your team? Is it welcomed or suppressed? Do you share this position or resist it?

vi) Shut your eyes for a few seconds and imagine a Warrior figure, a figure which embodies fierce conviction and commitment. What do you think about them? Would you trust this imagined figure?

vii) Now read over and assess your answers to the above questions. Can you see a general pattern of response emerging?

viii) If so, is it clear where this pattern of response came from? Like many inner voices, these responses may have started for excellent reasons. See if you can identify the causes of your current projections around the energy of the Warrior. What in your life so far could be a cause of this pattern?

Often, those who lack this energy are convinced that others will not like them if they become more assertive. In reality, usually exactly the opposite is true. Whenever somebody asserts themselves confidently, other people almost always find this very appealing, and often exciting. If you feel that a particularly strong inner voice is preventing you appreciating the assertiveness of the Warrior, you may want to return to the "Inner Coach" exercise to help you. If and when you are ready, try the exercise below.

Exercise 9d: Developing Assertiveness

i) Find a friend or colleague that you trust. Explain that you are trying to develop assertiveness and ask them if they will be your "buddy".

ii) If they are up for it, ask them to let you know – in real time – when they think you could be more assertive, both in your relationship with them and in other situations they witness. Then try it (at the next opportunity), and get their feedback. Hearing them appreciate your efforts will be the best possible antidote to the Inner Critic who tells you that being assertive will cause you to be disliked.

Another common obstacle is a lack of physical energy and/or a general discomfort with the physical power of the Warrior. The Warrior is a dynamic character, and has a high level of energy running through his body. Some people naturally have more access to that kind of energy. These are people who enjoy sport or hard work-outs in the gym. As children their physical energy was probably welcomed and enjoyed by their parents and primary carers.

Some people have a different experience, as you may have identified in Exercise 9c). Perhaps your physicality was not appreciated, perhaps you were sometimes made to feel "wrong" about your energy and assertiveness, as was Lin. If this, or any variation of it, is true for you then you may find it helpful to make a commitment to an activity that will allow you to experience the power of strong physical energy.

> As a teacher of acting and personal development workshop leader, Nicholas was very comfortable having impact and being assertive in front of small groups of 15–30 people. However:
>
> "When I first started presenting to groups of over a hundred people I found it difficult to extend my energy to have the same impact in a big group as I could in a small group. I looked around for a powerful form of exercise that I could do at short notice in small spaces (like hotel rooms). I chose Ashtanga Yoga – known as 'Power Yoga' – found a personal coach and worked at it until I knew a simple routine off by heart. Now every time I know I will be delivering to a large group I do a 30–40 minute session first thing in the morning. It's still tough and I have to consciously call in the Warrior to force myself to get up and do it, but it always pays off. Later on in the day, standing in front of the group, I can still feel the energy in my body. It allows me to command the space and project powerfully to the whole room."

When you come to formulate an action plan to develop this character, bear in mind the choice of an appropriate physical activity.

DEVELOPING THE WARRIOR

As with the other characters, you can also call up in your imagination real and fictional figures which carry this energy.

Exercise 9e: Finding Positive Images of the Warrior

i) Personal role models – think of people that you personally know and respect, and who exhibit dynamic assertive energy. Make a list of them and the qualities you admire in them.

ii) Public role models – think of people in the public eye (past or present) whom you may never meet, but whom you recognize as using Warrior qualities effectively. Some examples: Martin Luther King, the Second World War spitfire pilot Douglas Bader, Winston Churchill ("We will fight them on the beaches..."), marathon runners, Lance Armstrong, mountaineers/ explorers, the New York firemen on 9/11, Bob Geldof (with "Live Aid").

iii) Fictional role models – characters from works of fiction and/or the actors who play these parts particularly well. Examples: Sigourney Weaver in *Alien*, Mel Gibson in *Braveheart*, Luke Skywalker, Robin Hood, Bruce Willis in *Die Hard* and any other favourite action heroes who defy the odds to achieve their goals.

Next is an exercise to help you find an internal image and resource. This, again, will be accessed through an Active Imagination, or a guided "waking dream".

Exercise 9f: Active Imagination to find the Warrior

For this exercise you will need 10–15 minutes undisturbed – with pen and paper. Read through the directions until you are familiar enough with the process to start by yourself; it is better to go all the way through the journey without stopping, if you can.

i) Close your eyes and relax. Let all your thoughts and worries disappear. Imagine with your inner eye that you can now "levitate" your body. Imagine yourself floating upwards, moving through ceilings, floors and air as necessary until you are high in the sky. Now imagine yourself flying very fast across landscapes and over water.

ii) Now imagine you are coming down to land on a rugged, wind-swept mountain. Stand in this environment and feel the power of the natural elements. This is the home of the Warrior. Simply to have got this far will have required great perseverance on his part.

iii) Now imagine a Warrior walking towards you. What does he look like? How does he carry himself? What kind of energy emanates from him?

iv) Have a brief interaction; observe him carefully – how he acts, talks and engages with you. Feel his power.

v) When you are ready, take your leave and retrace your steps. Imagine flying back over water and landscapes until you arrive back in the room you started from. Stretch slowly and open your eyes.

vi) As soon as you are ready, write a record of your Active Imagination journey.

By now you should have a few different, positive images of a Warrior to work with. These are your resources to bring to rehearsal.

Exercise 9g: Rehearsal – Becoming the Image

This exercise will take 10–15 minutes undisturbed in a room large enough to move about in and containing a stick/broom handle.

i) Look through your notes from 9e) and f). Select the image of a Warrior that you feel to be the right one to rehearse "becoming" – you can always change your mind or try a few different ones later.

ii) Lie down on the floor and practise some diaphragm breathing. Relax and let your mind empty. When you are ready, see a corridor in your mind's eye, stretching out in front of you into the distance. Imagine that there is an entrance into the corridor at the far end where someone could enter into your line of vision. Know that the Warrior you have chosen to work with is waiting just out of your sight, at the end of the corridor.

iii) When you are ready, "allow" this Warrior to appear at the end of the corridor and let this figure begin to move towards you. Watch the figure carefully. Examine how they walk, how they move and how they hold themselves. Allow them to keep moving towards you until they are very close, imagine them greeting you and listen to how they sound embodying their natural power and focus.

iv) When you are ready, imagine this figure turning round and backing into your actual body, as if it were a spirit entering a physical form. Imagine how your body would feel different if this figure were actually within you. How would it change the way you think, feel, move and talk?

v) When you are ready, allow yourself to get up and stand, as if you were now the figure. Try and feel the difference between how you stand now and how you normally stand. Allow yourself imaginatively to "become" the image, and practise moving about like the figure moved in your imagination. Practise walking, standing, holding the stick as if it were a sword or lance, and speaking, in the manner of the figure you have chosen to rehearse. If you try anything that doesn't work for you, or feels out of character with the Warrior, simply stop and try something else. There is no failure in a rehearsal, only learning opportunities. Continue rehearsing for as long as you feel is useful.

vi) Make a few notes about how you felt, what worked and what didn't.

The more you are able to practise and rehearse, the more comfortable you will become bringing this character into your presentation style and content.

CUES
As with each of the characters there are certain ways of being and talking that characterize the Warrior. Practising these cues will also help you make the character more familiar.

THE WARRIOR – DYNAMIC MASCULINE
Gives a "call to arms".

POSTURE
Standing, upright, strong, energized, "animal prowling".

GESTURES
Forceful, direct, staccato, urgent, energetic, animated, rousing, strong eye contact, passionate.

VOCAL TONE
Committed, impassioned, fierce, carries conviction, fast, upbeat, loud, positive.

WORDS AND PHRASES
Short, quick sentences. Simple, punchy.

- "We must…" "We will"
- "The goal is within our grasp… one more push"
- "We can do it"
- "It will take…"
- "We will require…"
- "This is what we are going to do. This is how we are going to do it"
- "I want you to…"
- "Let's go!"

Now, if you wish, you can rehearse the cues.

Exercise 9h: Rehearsing the Cues

You will need 10–15 minutes in a room large enough to imagine giving a presentation in. You can do this exercise by yourself, using a mirror to observe yourself, or use feedback from a colleague whose opinion you trust.

i) Look over the above "cues" list and pick one or two ideas to practise from each heading.

ii) Imagine that you are about to start a presentation. Now "enter" and begin your presentation using the Warrior cues – you only need 15–30 seconds of material.

iii) Assess your performance – how was it? Did it work? Was it believable enough for you and/or your colleague? What do you want to try differently next time?

iv) Repeat until you feel you have "claimed" the attributes you are rehearsing.

These attributes should now be more available to you when you wish to call on them. You have a body memory of rehearsing the cues, which will give you the inner confidence to be more powerful and assertive the next time you give a presentation which calls for the Warrior.

ACTIVITIES TO PRACTISE THE WARRIOR

As in the previous chapters, overleaf is a list of activities to develop the character. Choose one of them, and make a commitment to practise it on a regular basis. Five to 10 minutes a day, or one hour a week, or a half-day every month is fine. The important thing is to pick something that you can consistently "rehearse" and that you know you will still be doing in six weeks to three months. Make the time commitment realistic or you will probably give it up before it has time to make a difference for you.

Warrior Activities

> Competitive sports
> Working out – gym
> Martial Arts – karate
> Punch bag
> Physical tasks/targets
> "Extreme" sports
> Archery, shooting
> Mountaineering
> Ashtanga Yoga
> Rock music.

Remember to do this activity in the spirit of the Warrior. It won't serve you to go to the gym for a work-out but turn up late and end up relaxing in the jacuzzi! At least not until you have worked hard, and pushed through some barriers first. Keeping the commitment to the activity is in itself a Warrior characteristic.

Exercise 9i: Choosing a Warrior Activity

Read through the above list and choose one activity you do not currently engage in that you think will help you get to grips with Warrior energy. Commit to practising it as and when your schedule allows. Make notes in your journal as to your progress and growing ease (or not) with the activity.

WARRIOR ACTION PLAN

If you have identified this character as your "learning edge" you may already have started practising some or all of the exercises in this chapter.

Wherever you have got to we would encourage you to look back through the chapter and draw up a simple action plan.

Exercise 9j: Warrior Action Plan

i) Which exercises, rehearsals and/or activities are you going to practise?

ii) When and where are you going to practise?

iii) How many times?

iv) Do you have a clear goal for these practices? How will you know when you have achieved this goal?

v) Do you want feedback from a trusted colleague? If so, who will you ask?

We all have a Warrior within us. As you get more in touch with him he will bring fiery and inspiring qualities to your presentations. Enjoy his (or rather your) vitality!

PART 4

Hitting the Mark

Chapter 10

Authenticity

*"Some people will like me and some people won't. So I might as well be myself, and then at least I'll know that the people who like me, like **me**!"*

Hugh Prather

If people can't "see" who you are when you are presenting they will not listen to you, and if you can't perform the role you are required to play in that presentation task well they will not listen to you! When you are being yourself and performing well they will listen to you for hours – "authentic" performance. In the last Part, "Expanding the Repertoire", we asked you to stretch beyond your usual "character" and learn how to play different roles. This is the "outside-in" approach; find an image "out there", learn how to play it and move it "in here" for appropriate performance. In this chapter we will focus on the "inside-out" approach, finding authenticity "in here" and then projecting it out into a room so that it becomes visible and compelling "out there".

Authenticity is about being yourself and not being afraid to show others who you are – being real, being you. This can be as simple as making one statement about your interest in what you are presenting. When you speak authentically you "show up" in the presentation; people notice this, and pay more attention. When you simply present facts, figures and company spin they turn off and stop listening.

LEVELS OF AUTHENTICITY

There are different levels of authenticity. Some are easier to access than others. At a simple level it can simply mean being real; acknowledging part of the reality of the situation that we would normally conceal, eg the terror some people feel when they forget an important point in a presentation. Some folk go into a trauma. Others can simply admit it;

"You know what, I've completely forgotten what I was going to say next. I'm just going to check my notes…" Nothing wrong with that. True, honest and authentically human in not being perfect. Next time someone asks you a difficult question after a presentation, don't pretend that you know the answer, if you don't. Simply acknowledge what is true, something like "Good question. I don't have that information right now. I'll get back to you." This kind of authentic response wins sympathy and understanding from an audience.

A deeper level of authenticity comes with finding a moment within a presentation to share our real connection with what we are saying, and why we are saying it. Sometimes it is appropriate to acknowledge our genuine emotional responses.

> Jim was a store manager for a big retail chain whose recent promotion was taking him from England to Ireland. On his arrival he would be required to make a speech to his new staff; he wanted to make a good impression. He started off his coaching session with what he thought was expected of him; "I am indeed very pleased to be standing in front of you today. I am confident that this will prove a successful venture for all of us. I am sure we will be able to increase revenue over the first year and continue steady growth thereafter…"
>
> His audience reported that it was OK, sensible enough, but a bit obvious. We fed back to Jim that his presentation came across as well-meaning but elaborate spin. So we asked him to reflect about his real thoughts and feelings. Forget what he thought he ought to say. What did he genuinely care about that he could link to his work?
>
> Jim paired up with another participant who took notes as he talked through his authentic reactions to the situation. Then we simply asked him to tell us what was true for him, as the unique human being Jim. Take Two was very different:
>
> "I believe in collaboration. My experience is that when people come together in a spirit of trust almost anything is possible. I want us to work on building that trust and on developing more collaboration across teams and departments. I am also extremely pleased to be here, in this land. I feel very committed to working in this community. My grandmother was born

in Ireland and I have always wanted to spend some time in the country of my ancestors. The level of welcome and warmth I have felt in the short time I have been here has meant a lot to me. In a way I would say that everything in my career up to now has prepared me for this step, and I am looking forward to every minute of it."

Even as he was speaking, his audience began smiling. He had engaged them by being authentic.

Notice how the personal touch draws us in. Often we think it is the redundant bit. Actually, it is the heart and soul. Remember Martin Luther King's last picture in his famous speech: "I have a dream that my four little children will one day live in a nation where they will not be judged by the colour of their skin but by the content of their character."

That is what was in it for him, a personal ambition and dream within a massive cultural and racial struggle. But we have never yet heard anyone complain; "That's a bit selfish – doing all this, just for his kids!" It is the deeply felt personal wish that helps make it universally appealing. We don't have to have four children to understand his dream; it is authentic and it has impact.

THE MASK

This deeper level of showing others who we really are and what we really care about can be more difficult to access. Many of us are not used to showing this much of ourselves at work. Most of us go about most working days wearing a very carefully constructed mask – constructed, in fact, precisely to hide who we really are from others.

Often this is necessary because – if truth be told – we left a little bit of our real selves at home, and a bit more in the car park or on the bus. As a colleague of ours recently told a conference audience listening to his presentation on Emotional Intelligence; "Rumour has it that some of you are having a near-life experience!" Since they didn't walk out, we can only surmise they intuitively knew what he was talking about. The chances are that they were holding something back. We often think we

"Wearing a Screen Saver Face"

are just holding this "something" back from our employer, but most of us end up holding the same something back from ourselves as well.

One of our favourite poems speaks about this:

I HAVE ARRIVED

I have not seen the plays in town,
only the computer printouts
I have not read the latest books
only the Wall Street Journal
I have not heard the birds sing this year

only the ringing of phones
I have not taken a walk anywhere
but from the parking lot to the office
I have not shared a feeling in years
but my thoughts are known to all
I have not listened to my own needs
but what I want I get
I have not shed a tear in ages
I have arrived.
Is this where I was going?

(Natasha Josefowitz)

This is a big question, and for us prompts a follow-up; who was it exactly that had "arrived" while not sharing any feelings or listening to their own needs? Maybe it was an automaton rather than a whole person, a human "doing" rather than a human being, a person wearing an effective mask. The pressure to meet the target and get the next promotion can focus us so exclusively and compellingly on the what "out there" that we forget to focus on the who "in here".

It's a common condition. As John Lennon once remarked; "Life is what happens while you're busy making other plans." There are many reasons in our life why we might not really be ourselves, especially at work. Deep down we may feel that we don't quite know who we are. Some jobs seem not to require all of us anyway; we can do most of it "on automatic". Or we don't really care about what we do; "It's just a job, just a way to put bread on the table." Sometimes our full selves – personal opinions, moods, variable emotions and all – can seem to interfere with simply getting on with the task in hand. So we "put a face on it" and wear a mask, the apparently presentable version of who we choose to be and what we decide to reveal at work.

On some people the mask is more obvious than others – those with a permanent smile plastered on their face, for example – you know they can't *really* want to smile that much. On others it is subtler, more layered, more a result of years of experience – reading spoken and unspoken messages around them about what is and is not acceptable to show in their company's culture.

And let's face it, sometimes the mask has been essential to our survival. It got us through that terrible day, or helped us keep our sanity during *that* project, or hold our tongue while working for that boss – or whatever. Who knows, it may be important again. But – and this is a BIG BUT – the habitual mask will not help you make a truly impactful presentation, in fact it will almost certainly get in the way. Not for everyone and not every time (the old saying "You can fool some of the people some of the time" has some truth in it), but usually the mask will be an unhelpful barrier between you and your audience.

DEVELOPING AWARENESS

So we don't suggest that you throw the mask away, rather that you become more aware of it. Awareness is the beginning of change. As you become more conscious of the mask you will begin to be able to choose when to wear it and when to drop it. This is a big step. At the beginning it will be tough; you've lived with it for a long time and often will not notice it, but with practice you will. As the psychologist RD Laing once observed; "The range of what we think and do is limited by what we fail to notice. And because we fail to notice that we fail to notice, there is little we can do to change – until we notice how failing to notice shapes our thoughts and deeds."

The forgetting becomes unconscious and habitual, so some conscious attention to remembering is required. Actually, of course, since the problem is that we forget that we have forgotten, the solution is to remember to remember! The Spanish poet Juan Ramon Jimenez wrote about the difference between the "I" we present to the world and the deeper, more authentic "I" of our true selves:

I AM NOT I

I am not I,
I am this one walking beside me

Whom I do not see,
Whom at times I manage to visit,
But usually I forget.
The one who remains silent when I talk,
The one who forgives, sweet, when I hate,
The one who takes a walk when I am indoors,
The one who will remain standing when I die.

(Translated by Robert Bly)

As we develop authenticity we will make more frequent visits to that other "I" walking beside us, the one we usually forget. A word of warning; the masks we wear have taken years to construct, they will not dissolve because you read a few pages of this book or do an exercise once or twice. Much of what we talk about in this chapter cannot be rushed and have any lasting effect. Take your time with the following exercises. Even if you choose to read on now to the end of the book, come back to these exercises; unless, of course, you have already done some work around developing authenticity elsewhere and are confident of your ability to present in a way that reveals who you are and what you care about to others.

Exercise 10a: Daily Reflection

i) Sit down quietly, for five minutes, at the end of a busy day and reflect on your "mask work" that day. Can you remember those times when, deep down, you felt there was something else – more genuine, more authentic – that could have been said, but, in the moment, you took what may have felt like an easier option?

ii) Can you recall when, where and why you responded from the mask rather than from your authentic self? Try not to be judgemental, simply develop your awareness. There is no right or wrong answer, only what was true for you, on that day.

iii) Jot down a few notes in your journal.

Exercise 10b: Pattern Recognition

i) When you have engaged in Exercise 10a) for a week or two, pay attention to what patterns begin to emerge in your observations. Does the mask tend to appear at a particular time of day? When faced with a particular kind of challenge, or person? (This will be especially useful information if you are ever called to give a presentation at this time, about these kinds of challenges, to these people...)

Exercise 10c: Remembering to Remember

i) Think about some activities that could help you "remember to remember". (This is a development of an early Presence exercise so it may be familiar.) Think through your average daily schedule. Think of a few actions you will generally engage in several times a day – having a cup of coffee, turning on a computer, looking in the mirror, walking up stairs etc.

ii) Choose one you are prepared to use as a conscious "trigger". Commit to using this activity as a cue to yourself to raise your awareness.

iii) Every time you engage in this activity simply reflect on your level of authenticity since the last cue. In your last few interactions were you being authentic or presenting a mask – or some combination of both?

iv) Try and be more authentic between now and the next cue. Notice how increased awareness of the mask can make you more authentically Present during your working day.

v) If you practise these exercises for a while you will eventually become aware of how and when you wear the mask. You might even become aware of the moment some part of you chooses to use the mask. Try and catch what the "inner voice" is saying at these moments. Write it down.

ASSUMPTIONS AND COUNTER-ARGUMENTS

Implicit in the notion of a mask is that there is some reason why we should not just be ourselves. But as we have found with many of the other "inner voices" we have encountered on the journey so far, many of these "reasons" are outdated and unnecessary obstacles to us having impact in public.

> Richard is now used to presenting for large audiences but recently has had to engage in meetings with potentially important clients:
>
> "The mask often appears when I am trying to be liked, especially in the presence of 'important' strangers, like new clients. My inner voice repeatedly tells me 'Be nice, be careful, don't give them an excuse to turn off or go away.' Over time it has probably been useful, but now the clients I most want to work with are those interested in bringing authenticity into their leadership culture. If I simply listen to the old assumptions of the inner voice and put on the 'nice' mask, I would blow it; they would leave thinking we were not the right people to work with after all."

So, if we are to develop a degree of choice about when and where to wear the mask, it will be important to question the assumptions that prompt us to don the mask. One of the most effective ways to do this is by consciously developing a counter-argument to the assumption.

Richard's habitual assumption, "Better be nice, could be big business!", can be neutralized by a new perspective, "Hang on, they are talking about developing authenticity in their leadership team; if you can't be who you really are with them they won't want you, however nice you appear!"

So see if you can identify the assumption behind the mask and develop a counter-argument to it.

Exercise 10d: Assumptions and Counter-arguments

i) Identify the "inner voice" – what are you thinking when you put on the mask? What are the assumptions about why it is necessary, or better, easier etc?

ii) Write them down in your journal.

iii) Now check; in retrospect, do you agree with the assumption the voice made? If so, fine, it was probably the right choice in that moment. If not, how would you argue the other side? Write it down. Try and remember it.

iv) Next time you notice the temptation to "mask up", listen to the voice of habitual assumption and then answer it with this new perspective.

v) At this point you can make a judgement call. Which feels right? If, on balance, the old voice wins, then mask up and good luck. If not, pursue the authentic option and see how it goes.

vi) Note down your experiences in your journal.

There is usually a moment of risk or anxiety before making the more authentic choice. This is natural. It is only by "feeling the fear and doing it anyway" that you can break through to this deeper level of authenticity and impact.

> Nicholas was presenting "The Art of Leading Change with *The Tempest*" to a room full of financial analysts for a large investment company:
>
> "They were a potentially important new client, with several directors in the room. I was about 15 minutes into a 90-minute presentation when I noticed several young men in the back row drumming their fingers and looking at the clock, obviously not engaged. I was just about to go into a big speech from the play, but knew intuitively that this would not engage these people. I had a choice – do the performance I usually do and know most people will like it, or drop into a deeper level of authenticity. I became momentarily nervous; if I challenged them with a deeper level of authenticity some of the directors who enjoyed the Shakespeare performance might be put off. I decided to take the risk. 'Look, I know there are probably people here who think listening to Shakespeare is a waste of time. But this isn't about Shakespeare, this is about what you make of your working life. When you get to your retirement day are you are going to look back and say *God, what was I doing all those years?!* Or are you going to be able to look back and say *That was a good deal – I lived my potential.*' The drumming on the table stopped. Because I had dropped the 'Shakespeare performance mask', and said what I really believed in, they were suddenly engaged in a different way. What took me through the fear barrier was being able to call on the things I really care about. I want myself and others to get meaning out of work. It was drawing on that genuine passion that gave me the courage to risk not being liked."

Which brings us to a couple of important questions... Are you clear about what you really care about? Do you currently live your core values at work?

CORE VALUES

The 2002 film *Adaptations*, starring Nicolas Cage, contains the line; "You are what you love, not what loves you." Authenticity demands a combination of thought and feeling, logic and caring, what you think and what you stand for. Are you clear about what you stand for? It is an important route towards the authentic self. We know from experience that such questions can seem embarrassing or even unnecessary at first, but we encourage you to try it and see.

Exercise 10e: Core Values in Life and Work

This exercise will take 20–30 minutes with journal and pen.
i) Make a list of what you care most about in the world. Add a list of your personal values. What do you stand for? What are you prepared to stand up for? What are you prepared to stand against?
ii) When you have finished, read through it. How do you feel as you read the list? Does it reflect (at least) a part of who you are?
iii) Now turn your mind to work. Write a list of what you most care about in what you do at work. Now turn your mind to your organization. What is it that your organization does, or contributes to, that you are proud of?
iv) Now reflect on two or three of your peak working experiences. When have you felt happiest at work? When has your work had the most meaning for you? What was happening? What was going on at those times that made them better than others? What conditions were operating that created these peak working experiences? Make a list for each peak working experience.
v) Now find the common denominators. Which conditions were common for most or all of your peak experiences? Then read through that list. Do these conditions give you a sense of meaningful work?
vi) Notice how many of these conditions are true of your current situation. The more you have, the more likely you will be able to be authentic in your current environment.

The fact is, you will be much more likely to be authentic if you can relate a presentation – however tangentially – to something that you care about. Your attachment to the outcome will help you to "show up" and engage others. A survey in the US discovered that those who were happiest in their work had made a direct connection between their personal values and their company's mission or vision. We recommend that you apply the same principle to your presentations. What is it that you are required to say that you most believe in? If the answer is "nothing much" you've got some work to do!

Of course, sometimes we may be asked to do things we don't quite believe in – or think are not in line with our core values. This is tricky. If you simply fake it, and project something you do not believe, you will end up in trouble. You will feel inauthentic, and once others spot that inauthenticity they lose trust in you. Trust can take a lifetime to build but 10 minutes to destroy. You can get through it with integrity if you can find something in the situation you genuinely believe in, that does bring you authentically Present.

> We were coaching Bill, a senior manager from a major telecommunications company, who had been tasked with downsizing his department of 3,000 engineers by 10%. The problem was, he was a natural Great Mother, a "people person" who had built up this department from scratch over 15 years and now felt that he was being told to axe 300 friends at the whim of a chairman responding to shareholder pressure. He did not feel connected to what he was being asked to do. He was seriously wondering about leaving himself.
>
> We worked with him to establish his core values in life and work, and to balance up the pros and cons of doing what he had been told to do or choosing to leave the company. After some considered reflection he decided to stay, mainly because of the 2,700 people who would be left, and also because his people-centred approach would be more likely to make the downsizing as painless as possible for everyone concerned.
>
> Now we had to work out how he could present the situation to his people without lying or being inauthentic. He couldn't go out and blame the chairman, or say how wrong he thought it was to the 3,000 engineers. In the end he worked out two parallel strategies, one for the 30 members of

the Senior Management Team – who knew him best – another for the other 2,970.

To the managers closest to him he could be completely authentic: "Listen, guys, you know me. This is the last thing I wanted to happen. But I've thought through it and I have decided to stay and see it through. I am asking you to help me. We are in the best position to do this as well as possible and cause the least pain and disruption for all our people, both those who leave and those who stay."

To the others he had to take more of the company line, but he still had to stand on his values to maintain authenticity in this more public arena:

"You've all heard the bad news about the 10% redundancy. I'm sorry to have to lose some of you but it is for the overall good of the company, and will ensure our survival in the long term. I do want to give you a few personal reassurances. I will do whatever I can to ensure that there are no compulsory redundancies. I will fight for the best packages possible, and I guarantee that they will include retraining, for those who wish it. I give you my personal commitment that if we can turn this company around in the next couple of years, and jobs become available, you guys will be the first on my list. And I want you to know that my door is open. Anyone who has concerns can talk to me personally, and I will do my best to address them."

By bringing himself in and talking about the things he most cared about in the situation he could maintain authenticity and trust within an extremely tense and difficult presentation task.

We often find it takes a while for people to identify what they really care about. Often there is a layer of what people think they ought to care about that gets in the way.

WHAT REALLY MATTERS

A good friend and colleague of ours, the poet-philosopher David Whyte, has developed a writing exercise that guides people towards what really matters to them. One that cuts through the "ought to's" and gets to a few home truths. It is based on one of his poems:

SELF-PORTRAIT

It doesn't interest me if there is one God
or many gods.
I want to know if you belong or feel abandoned.
If you know despair or can see it in others.
I want to know
if you are prepared to live in the world
with its harsh need
to change you. If you can look back
with firm eyes
saying this is where I stand. I want to know
if you know
how to melt the fierce heat of living
falling toward
the centre of your longing. I want to know
if you are wiling to live, day by day,
with the consequence of love
and the bitter
unwanted passion of your sure defeat.

I have been told, in that fierce embrace, even
the gods speak of God.

One participant in a writing workshop came up with her own version; it started like this:

"It doesn't interest me what you do for a living. I want to know what you ache for, and if you dare to dream of meeting your heart's longing...

It doesn't interest me if the story you are telling me is true. I want to know if you can disappoint another to be true to yourself; if you can bear the accusation of betrayal and not betray your own soul; if you can be faithless and therefore trustworthy..."

(By "Oriah Mountain Dreamer")

You may have come across this in some form; it was popular on the e-mail circuit a few years back and has become the basis of a best-selling book. Now it's your turn...

Exercise 10f: "It Doesn't Interest Me If... I Want To Know"

You will need 15–20 minutes undisturbed, with journal and pen.
i) Simply start writing a sentence that begins "It doesn't interest me if..." and see how you want to continue, then add "I want to know..." and finish the sentence in your own way. Continue this until you run out of ideas.
ii) Now read it over. Is it true? If not, simply rewrite it until you are satisfied it reflects the real you.

If it takes a while to get through the barriers and filters, draw comfort from the words of that inspirational speaker Winston Churchill; "Writing is 1% inspiration and 99% perspiration!" When you are ready, you will have created the raw material for your next rehearsal exercise – sharing what you have written with a trusted friend or colleague. Like much of what we suggest, it is useful to do this outside of a pressured situation first. You can learn to become more comfortable with being authentic.

Exercise 10g: Communicating Authenticity

i) Who do you know that you trust enough to be willing to share this with? If no one springs to mind immediately, sit with the possibility for a while and decide later. If you've got a few choices pick someone (preferably not the CEO, at least as a first experiment) and find a time to try it out.
ii) Explain the nature of the exercise, if you wish, or simply buy them a drink and find a good time to share what you have written. Chances are it will be the beginning of an unusual, deep and authentic conversation.
iii) If your first choice is a friend or partner outside of work, and it goes well, then think about who you would be willing to share it with inside your working environment. Then try it out. Be courageous. What have you got to lose – apart from the mask?
Warning: It is best to avoid compulsive jokers and cynics who think poetry and personal development is a load of rubbish.

The next test is to find a presentation opportunity where you can show more of yourself than you would normally be prepared to do. Tom Chappell, CEO of Tom's of Maine (producers of "natural care" products), welcomes this kind of authenticity:

> "The triumph of the mission – and its joy – is that we are being ourselves in running the business. Our knowledge that our values matter keeps reinforcing our identity, sharpening our competitive edge. But if our souls aren't on the journey, if our quest is only about figuring out another plan, it will be just another strategy, just another plan, just another game. Living and working are too important to let that happen."

So how can you get your soul on the journey? How can you be more authentic in an upcoming presentation?

Exercise 10h: Practising Authenticity in Presentations

You may want to find a colleague to rehearse this with first, or you may just choose to stand up and practise in public. Unfortunately – or perhaps fortunately – you need to figure out how you are going to show more authenticity. If we told you, or prescribed a method, it would be a method, someone else's idea, and therefore *not* authentic, not from inside you. Take your time, choose your place and have a go...

Chapter 11

Preparing for Peak Performance

In this final chapter we will help you prepare for Peak Performance Presentations. So far we have examined in detail the different elements that create effective performance – now is the time to bring these elements together.

What preparation do you need to give yourself the best opportunity of achieving Peak Performance?

When you find the right preparation for you, you will know it and you will see and feel the difference. The great cellist Yo-Yo Ma spends up to an hour onstage before a concert moving his seat inches left and right until he finds the exact spot where he and his instrument feel most attuned. When we go to the theatre or attend a conference, do we not want the performers to have made every effort to ensure that they give their best?

Yet, as we have noted before, most corporate speakers devote all available time to preparing their material, rather than preparing themselves. A colleague of ours recently worked out that at international conferences each half-hour presentation may cost an organization something like £50,000 (or $90,000). He then asks; "Are you worth your 50 grand?" We would add; Are you taking your preparation seriously enough?

"I'M TOO BUSY"

Given the speed and pressure of working life, it is easy to say "I don't have time, I'm too busy." But as an approach to achieving Peak Performance it is a poor excuse. You may know the old story about sharpening your axe:

> A man walking in a forest comes across a woodcutter chopping down trees. As he gets nearer he sees how hard the woodcutter is working, and how exhausting the work is. Moreover, it soon becomes clear that the axe he is using is blunt. So he talks to the woodcutter and says; "You know, if you

walk down that path over there for about 15 minutes there's a man who can sharpen your axe." Barely looking at him, the woodcutter replies; "Good God, I haven't got time for that. I've got far too much work to do!"

Your preparation is the key to starting a presentation with a "sharp axe". When you take the time, the benefits become obvious – to you and your audience. When we are well-prepared, and Present, we always achieve much better results.

Mahatma Gandhi was once asked how he prepared himself for the pressure of leadership. He replied: "I meditate for an hour every morning, before I start work." The interviewer then asked, "But surely there must be some days when the pressure is so intense that you can't stick to your normal routine. What do you do then?" "Ah," said Gandhi, "on those days I get up an hour earlier and meditate for two hours."

Recent studies indicate that "chill out" rooms onsite, where people can go and relax for a short while during a working day, increase productivity. The "loss" of 15 minutes' work time is repaid with greater overall efficiency and effectiveness. The same is true of presentations. As they say; "Fail to prepare, prepare to fail."

We will take you through all the different aspects of effective preparation, starting with the most practical outer elements and then reminding you of inner preparation possibilities. Along the way we will give you examples of what we (and others) do. We will then suggest a 10-minute sequence you can use to prepare yourself before any future presentation. Once you have tried the different options, we advise you to select the elements that work best for you, and design your own sequence.

PART 1 – EXTERNAL PREPARATION

We strongly recommend an advance visit to the location in which you will be speaking. Most of the keys to Peak Performance lie within you, but no good actor ever walks onto a stage for the first time, in front of a paying audience, without having checked the physical space beforehand. You too can take into account the unique layout of the specific place in which you will present. Whether it is a small meeting room or a large conference hall, knowing the space will make you more confident and better prepared.

Cover as many of the following points as possible:

- What is the physical layout of the stage or area from which you will present? Specifically, how is the technology set up? Is it where you want it? More often than not there is an assumption that the PowerPoint or OHP is the most important aspect of the presentation, so it will dominate the stage. We always try to ensure that any projection screen is at the side, so we, the presenter/s, occupy centre stage. Be sure that the technology is supporting the impact you want to make.

Richard was giving a keynote presentation to a group of chief executives at a local government conference:

"I got into the room as early as I could, half an hour before the start time. The room was long and narrow. At the presenter's end there was a large PowerPoint screen dominating proceedings, with a lectern off in the corner. I knew I could not maintain interest and impact for 90 minutes in this set-up. I asked the technicians if they could move the screen to the side – they said No. I stood up front and looked about. If I used the PowerPoint in its current set-up I would not be able to move from behind the lectern without blocking the screen. I knew that the audience had a workbook containing all the slides from my presentation. I made my decision; cut the PowerPoint. Allow myself the space to move about and keep the audience engaged, referring them to the workbook when an important model was being discussed, rather than being pinned in a corner by technology. It worked fine – more importantly, I was much more comfortable and Present throughout."

- Check where you will be standing. Does it give you the best relationship with your audience? How are the sight lines (the audience's ability to see you clearly, and *vice versa*)? Do you need to be higher, so everyone at the back can see you? Do you have enough room to move around? On occasion you might conclude that the whole layout of the room needs to be changed.

Richard was working with a group from a South African business school on the last day of a three-day programme. The first two days of the course had required a lot of interaction among delegates and so they had sat around big round tables:

"When I arrived in the morning I saw that this layout meant that the group was stretched all the way to the back of a very large room. I stood at the front and looked at the set-up. It was not conducive to the intimate, personal atmosphere I wanted to create. So I asked the conference staff to take all the tables out and rearrange the chairs theatre style facing the long side of the room. They were just clocking off for breakfast at the time, and said they couldn't do it. I said I couldn't start until it was done. A brief chat with management did the trick. It was tight, time wise, but when we started the set-up suited the presentation, and the participants were better served."

- In a large venue, what kind of lighting will there be? When PowerPoint is used there is usually no light on stage, which does not serve your impact as a performer. We had a vivid reminder of this recently…

Richard and Nicholas were the speakers at a one-day conference for the Campaign for Leadership called "Pathways to Vision – in search of the creative leader":

"Since we had some input into the venue we chose a wonderful large space with a glass roof. When we arrived the day before for a rehearsal of the whole event, which also involved a small orchestra, we found that the technicians in charge of the PowerPoint had closed the roof. In order that the projection screen was more clearly visible, they had cancelled out the very reason we had chosen that venue. The context of the day required a more open atmosphere than most conference venues. We stuck to our guns. The roof remained open, beautiful sunlight streamed in on the day of the conference, and the spacious, airy atmosphere suited our subject matter in just the way we had hoped. While not every audience member could see the screen perfectly (they had the slides in a workbook anyway) they all got the experience that we had spent weeks designing and planning."

The key lesson in all of this is – *you are in charge.* Claim the right to have what you need as you want it. While you may not always be the most popular person in the technicians' corner, your job is not to please them. Your job is to give yourself and your audience the best experience you can. If all else fails, have your Inner Coach tell you "You deserve it, and the audience wants you to be at your best!"

Other important things to be aware of:

- Do you have a table for notes, water and a glass? Is it big enough? Is it in the right place?
- Check the entrance and exit if you will need to use them. Rehearse walking from your "offstage" starting place to your "onstage" starting place. Make sure that you will not encounter any unexpected obstacles, wires, door jams etc.
- Do a sound check. Practise your voice in the room. Speak a part of your presentation on the "stage", even if it's a small lecture theatre or boardroom. This serves several purposes. First, you get an idea of how your voice will sound in that particular space, so there will be no surprises at the actual event. Secondly, some spaces are very flat

acoustically. You can hear that there is no echo at all; you speak and the sound immediately stops. The same thing happens if you clap loudly. This means you will have to use more energy vocally, and it is good to know this beforehand.

- If it is a big space you will obviously need to speak louder. If possible, ask someone to go to the back of the room and check that you are clearly audible.

- If you are in any doubt about achieving comfortable audibility make sure a microphone will be available. We always ask for the clip-on variety, which allows us to move around freely. The advantage of a microphone is that it allows you to speak with a normal voice; you don't have to worry about being heard. If you will be using a mike insist on a sound check beforehand, and ask the technicians to use the lowest volume setting that achieves audibility. That way, your voice will still be clearly heard in all the speakers around the auditorium, but it will not sound unduly strange to you.

We both like to spend time in the room in which we will be presenting when we can, before the audience come in. Nicholas remarks: "I like to look out at the empty chairs, and then energetically 'take possession of the room'. It feels like making friends with the room, projecting my energy out into it, taking command of it. Sometimes I like to walk around the outside of the room to enhance the feeling. It's about feeling at home there."

- Wear comfortable clothes that are not restrictive, particularly around the neck and stomach areas. If you are wearing a tie make sure you choose a shirt with a loose enough neck. If you constrict your resonators your voice will sound tense.

- Drink weak black or herbal tea or room temperature water in the hour before you speak. Coffee heightens anxiety, milk creates mucous, ice tightens the vocal cords. Some people find that honey in a warm drink loosens their voice. Experiment until you find what suits you best.

PERSONAL "RITUALS"

Personal rituals are activities that help focus you. Some are logical, some apparently illogical – both can be important. Some actors make a ritual out of putting on their costumes. The feel of the material, its cut and shape, and finally how it looks, can play an important part in entering the world of the play and their "character". You can use clothes in this way. Whatever mood you may be in, putting on a well-tailored suit and high quality footwear may help you feel more ready. Choosing the right accessories – tie, jewellery etc – can help too. Stepping into your "costume" in a very deliberate way can help you make the transition from normal reality to performance mentality.

> Many performers from the Arts and Sport develop personal rituals to help prepare themselves for performance pressure. English footballer Paul Ince would always run out of the tunnel last, and only put his shirt on when he was on the pitch. The rugby player, Jonny Wilkinson, goes through an elaborate "ritual" before every kick: he always does the same hand actions, uses the same breathing patterns and glances at the posts – every time. It looks weird but it works for him. Golfers and tennis players develop sequences of actions they perform before every drive or serve. The best-selling author Michael Crichton (*Jurassic Park*, *ER*) remarked in an interview that whatever meal he eats on the day that he first starts a new book, he will then eat every day until the book is finished. He added: "I have another idiosyncrasy; there must be some clothes lying around somewhere in the room where I write. So I always keep a sweatshirt or gym clothes tossed on a chair in the corner. I have no idea why that is a requirement. But if the room is bare, I contrive to find something." All of these rituals serve to create an inner focus and readiness.

What do you currently do, if anything? Does it work? If not, you might want to experiment with one or two new personal preparation rituals.

PART 2 – INTERNAL PREPARATION

Now we are going to summarize the key learning points from previous chapters that can optimize your performance. We encourage you try them all and then choose which ones work best for you.

1 EMOTIONAL AWARENESS

Exercise 11a: Acknowledging Nerves and Emotion

Here you can use a combination of Presence, Inner Attention and Emotional Intelligence (Great Mother).

i) Close you eyes and "check in" with yourself. Pay attention to how you are feeling emotionally. At this point the most important thing is – DON'T TRY TO CHANGE ANYTHING. Just breathe, and pay attention. If you are feeling nervous, for example, pay attention to the exact feeling of those nerves.

ii) Notice where in your body you feel the sensation of "nervousness". Pay attention to precisely how it feels without trying to change it. Name the feeling to yourself as precisely as possible, and keep naming it each time it changes, however subtlely. Keep breathing easily, and paying attention.

As you learn to do this accurately you will find that your whole body/mind will quickly settle into a calm yet energized state of equilibrium. The energy of your emotional state will still be with you, but contained in a much more helpful way. The key is learning to trust the act of simply paying attention. When we are in a state we feel is unhelpful – particularly before an important performance – our natural impulse is to try to change or ignore that state. This very rarely works. Practise this different approach as often as you can. Try it whenever you sense an emotion stirring in you, or if you are feeling out of sorts. Just pay attention, keep your breathing flowing and keep naming the feeling. You will be amazed by what happens. Once you are used to it, you will find it will only take you a couple of minutes to settle yourself.

2 PRESENCE

For important presentations your inner preparation should start from the moment you wake up. You should aim to settle immediately into 50–50 awareness. This inner attention will reinforce your sense of "being" and enable you to pay the right attention to the different stages of your preparation, however fast you may have to be going in the lead-up to your performance.

Exercise 11b: Presence and Physical Awareness

i) If you have an exercise routine, do it as attentively as possible, breathing deeply. It is very worthwhile learning a few basic Yoga stretches. Doing these means you will already be settling into the feeling of being comfortable in your body, and you will also be opening up your energy.

ii) Check that your breathing is deep and rooted. Get as "grounded" as you can. Walk around. Settle into a high quality of attentiveness, both inner and outer.

iii) As you wash and get dressed, pay attention to breathing and the weight of your feet on the ground. As you eat chew your food more slowly than normal, pay attention to taste. If you walk outside, be aware of the air on your face, the wind, the smells, the sounds.

Different people use different ways to focus Presence and physical awareness.

Nicholas comments: "At home or, more likely, in my hotel room, I always take time on the day of a presentation to complete a 30-minute Yoga sequence. My personal preference is Ashtanga or Power Yoga. I make myself do it, even when I really don't feel like it. Within 10 minutes I am always very grateful I made the effort. It opens up my body and raises my whole energy level. It also awakens a strong degree of inner attention. After finishing the Yoga, I like to sit for five minutes' quiet meditation. I close my eyes and simply observe my breathing. It helps build the inner focus, and anchors a deep inner calm. As I go to breakfast I am already immersed in "The Practice of Presence" – Breathing, Grounding, Dual Attention. I am very conscious of everything and everyone around. I eat selectively, and less than usual. My personal preference is a high protein breakfast. I eat slowly. Everything is building towards the presentation. I feel like an arrow pointing itself in the required direction. When I arrive at the venue I know there will be a lot of activity, conversations etc. But I have anchored in myself the underlying feeling of Presence."

3 VOICE

Remember that your voice is a key instrument in how you come across to your audience. Time spent warming up this instrument is time well spent.

Exercise 11c: Vocal Warm-up

i) Massage your face. Loosen the jaw (1 minute).

ii) Align your body, head, shoulders and spine; get grounded, and breathing deeply (2 minutes).

iii) Use sounds "zzzzzzz", "sssssss", "haw" and "hoo". Breathe deeply, without lifting your shoulders (2 minutes).

iv) Use "The Elevator" exercise to find your natural note. Go from the "ah" sound into "Good morning, my name is..." and other simple sentences (2 minutes).

v) Speak some consonants, vowels, poetry or tongue twisters, getting faster and faster (1 minute).

vi) Speak some key sentences from your presentation (2 minutes).

4 OVERCOMING THE BLOCKS – INNER CRITIC/INNER COACH

You may also choose to reflect on the work you did with these figures. In particular:

Exercise 11d: Inner Coach

i) Remember an effective Inner Coach image. Imagine them with you, and listen to their words of advice and encouragement. Let the Coach's presence affect you as fully as you can, in both body and mind. Take a couple of deep breaths and let the feeling of support flow through you.

ii) Use any anchoring gestures or postures that you have found useful. If appropriate, use an object or item of clothing to reinforce the Coach.

Inner Coaches can help in even very stressful presentation situations.

We coached a UK public sector chief executive who had to speak to the nation's press at 10 Downing Street several times a year. She found this extremely intimidating, describing the press as "rottweilers". One of the things her Inner Coach gave her in the role-play session during the coaching was a suit of armour! She imagined putting this on, then stepping out in front of the press with this degree of protection. She found this very vivid, and very helpful. So we suggested that, next week, at Number 10, she should take a shawl with her. Just before the press conference she should ritually wrap it round her, as if she was putting on her suit of armour. We heard from her soon afterwards; it had worked a treat!

5 SENSE MEMORY

If you feel that you are not yet in the right frame of mind you might want to re-engage your Sense Memory (full version in Exercise 4a).

Exercise 11e: Sense Memory

i) Think through the places, activities and people that make you feel at your best.

ii) Bring them clearly to mind and let these images inform how you feel in the present moment.

6 CALLING IN A CHARACTER

What energy do you need to manifest for this presentation? If it is an energy that most naturally falls in the gift of one of your less favourite characters you might want to "summon" that character to be more fully present in you.

Exercise 11f: Summoning the Character

i) Look back to the following pages for a summary of each character's attributes: Good King, page 109; Great Mother, page 131; Medicine Woman, page 158; Warrior, page 173.

ii) Do whatever you need to generate the right feeling and energy inside you. Here are some suggestions:

Good King – visualize sitting on your throne; find the feeling of weight and gravitas in your body. Remember your Super Objective. Know you can achieve it.

Great Mother – think of someone you really care for. Let your heart open, and let the feeling spread inside you, softening and warming you. Imagine connecting with the audience you are about to speak to.

Medicine Woman – think of the art, music or poetry that inspires you.

Connect to your imagination and to the imagination of your audience. Remember the images, pictures and stories you are going to share with them. See them now, before you start.

Warrior – shadow box, punch the air, jump up and down, do whatever it takes to generate some physical energy. Think of your archetypal Warrior figure anchors. Let their energy come into you.

Let's see how one world-famous performer awakens a Great Mother feeling:

A colleague of ours went to see Tina Turner in concert, and had been invited to a reception with her afterwards. He had the opportunity to speak with her and asked: "How do you come out on stage and hold 40,000 people in the palm of your hand? How do you prepare yourself to do this?" "Honey," she replied, "let me tell you one of the most important things I do. When the audience are coming in I watch them from offstage. As I look at them all taking their seats, I say over and over again, 'I love you, I love you, I love you'. And when I come out onstage for the show that is what I am feeling. I am bursting with love for these people."

7 AUTHENTICITY

Make sure you don't forget to take off the mask. What is going to bring the real you most Present and able to achieve most impact?

Exercise 11g: Authenticity

i) Remember what connects you to your material. Call to mind your core values and personal sources of inspiration. Why are you doing this? What does it mean to you? What is it about the material that you can feel most connection with?

Different people will have different connections to their material.

Nicholas comments: "In this part of my preparation what works for me is a combination of Sense Memory and authenticity. I bring to mind a sacred place that I have visited within the last year or so. I close my eyes and visualize myself in that place. I feel the effect very quickly. It calms me, inspires me and elevates my spirit. Then I allow the reasons I do this work to come to my attention. At this point it is easy to remember what connects me to the material and what I am intending with the presentation. Finally, I imagine that the people I am about to address are also there in that place, so we are all enveloped in the same inspired atmosphere."

"WAITING IN THE WINGS" – PREPARATION SEQUENCE EXAMPLE

Not many people will have time to do all the above, although for particularly important presentations the more you can do the better. So let's imagine for now that you can find about 7–10 minutes in the hour or so before you are due to present. We will give you an example of a sequence we have found to be effective. As you gain more experience and confidence with the practice of preparation you will find your own unique variations and sequence.

Exercise 11h: Preparation Sequence Example

Ideally you need to have some privacy. This could be in the "wings" if you are on a stage at a conference, in your office if you are in your workplace, in an empty break out room at a conference venue – if all else fails, find a toilet and lock the door!

i) 2 minutes: Close your eyes and pay attention to exactly how you are feeling. Remember, don't try to change anything, just name and acknowledge.

ii) 1 minute: "The Practice of Presence". Breathe deeply, get really grounded, focus your Dual Attention.

iii) 2 minutes: Voice – massage your face, loosen your jaw. Do "The Elevator" exercise. Speak a few lines of your speech or a tongue twister.

iv) 2–5 minutes: Optimize your state by using any combination of Sense Memory, Inner Coach, Character and Authenticity images and exercises.

If you are unable to find time alone for this (maybe because you have to be on the stage at a conference or sitting in a meeting-room waiting to present next), you can learn to do your preparation internally. The only step that won't be possible is a vocal warm-up, so remember to do that before you enter the room; even if it means doing it hours before you will speak it will still help. When you are sitting in the conference room you simply withdraw most of your attention from the outside, concentrate on your breathing and go through the most important parts of your preparation in your mind's eye. Just bring the images into your imagination and let them inform your state appropriately. This is perfectly possible, with a little practice, and will become an invaluable tool to prepare you for many different situations.

STEPPING ONSTAGE

At a certain point, the rehearsals are over, the preparation is done, and the time to perform is upon us.

Exercise 11i: Stepping Onstage

As you are just about to start:

i) Settle in Dual Attention. If you are being introduced, stay very Present in yourself, and monitor the audience. Taking into account their state, you may need to alter how you begin.

ii) Make sure that when the introduction is over you move into position at your pace, in your rhythm.

iii) Once in position, settle yourself, breathe, ground yourself. You feel relaxed and alert, confident, authentic, Present. You are ready to begin!

Just as in the theatre, it is all the work you have done offstage, preparing and rehearsing, that you now have access to, in the moment, as you speak to the audience. The audience don't see the actors rehearse, your audience won't see you prepare, but they will get the benefit – Peak Performance.

As we say in theatre – "break a leg!"

Epilogue

"All the great possibilities unexplored in history and the thousand biographies of the great ones are but the beginning and the foundation of new ways of living, of working and dreaming one's way out of the corner we find ourselves in if we but choose life over death, hope over fear, a greater self-image over a smaller one."

Ben Okri, *In Arcadia*

We share a passionate interest in people living their full potential at work. As Carl Jung wrote; "Many people live their lives as if they were walking around in shoes that are too small for them." We have heard time and again how many organizations develop a culture of restricted behaviour – small shoes, small self-image – which inevitably gets reflected in less than inspiring presentations. Then their senior managers come to us wanting to achieve more powerful impact.

A couple of years ago Nicholas attended a conference in Scotland. On the first morning he sat through several keynote speeches. One was delivered by the Chief Executive of one of the UK's best-known public service organizations. Already a small woman, she stood, just visible, behind a lectern and read a 40-minute speech, word for word, hardly looking at the audience. Needless to say it was pretty dull. That evening at dinner Nicholas was placed next to her. They settled into an animated conversation about values in the workplace. She spoke with great passion and conviction. Feeling emboldened Nicholas asked if he might ask her a very direct question. She agreed. His question was; "Why, when you can speak in such a vital, captivating way, as you have been doing all through our conversation, did you deliver such a boring presentation this morning? In your presentations, why don't you stand right in the centre of the stage and speak with the effortless passion with which you have been speaking to me? You would be utterly captivating and inspirational if you did so." Her reply was; "I know. I'm longing to do exactly that, I just haven't quite got the courage."

She was right. Being a good presenter does take courage as well as technique. It is much easier and safer to hide behind your PowerPoint data than it is to stand and deliver a speech with authenticity, passion and imagination. To be inspirational and memorable means standing in the full power of your individuality. This is an act of daring as well as courage, and it sometimes means going against the stream.

Although coaching and training can provide the tools, in the end the change has to come from inside each individual. It is the power of the individual's own unique voice that carries the seed of inspiration. Most of us need and deserve bigger shoes! Once people see how much more impact they can achieve when they overcome their inhibitions and perform authentically, it is much easier to make the change stick. And it is clear that both individuals and organizations benefit from Peak Performance.

This is the time for all of us to bring more of ourselves to work. Many organizations are looking for that extra edge, be it of commitment, creativity or inspiration. Your presentations are one of the best places for you to embody these qualities. When you do so you help create a culture in which living your potential becomes the norm, rather than the exception. You become the example that others can follow. To quote Marianne Williamson:

> *...as we let our own light shine,*
> *we unconsciously give other people*
> *permission to do the same.*
> *As we are liberated from our fear,*
> *our presence automatically liberates others.*

We wish you a liberated future – where you can be truly Present, and let your light shine.

Bibliography/Further Reading

Autry, James. *Love and Profit*. Avon Books, 1991.

Ayot, William. *Small Things that Matter*. The Well Press, 2003 (only available through Olivier Mythodrama).

Bly, Robert (Editor). *Lorca and Jimenez: Selected poems*. Beacon Press, 1973.

Brook, Peter. *The Empty Space*. Touchstone Books, 1995.

Brook, Peter. *There are no Secrets*. Methuen, 1995.

Brook, Peter. *The Shifting Point 1946-1987*. HarperCollins, 1987.

Brook, Peter. *Threads of Time: Recollections*. Counterpoint Press, 1998.

Carr, Ian. *Keith Jarrett*. Da Capo Press, 1992.

Chekhov, Michael. *To the Actor*. Routledge, 2002.

Goleman, Daniel. *Working with Emotional Intelligence*. Bloomsbury, 1998.

Grotowski, Jerzy. *Towards a Poor Theatre*. Eyre Methuen, 1976.

Hastings, Robert. *The Station*. Tristan Publishing, 2003.

Hill, Gareth. *Masculine and Feminine*. Shambahala, 1992.

Hoffnung, Robert and Seifert, Kelvin. *Lifespan Development*. Houghton Mifflin, 1999.

Josefowitz, Natasha. *Is This Where I Was Going?* Warner Books, 1983.

Klein, Joe. *The Natural*. Broadway Books, 2002.

Kumiega, Jennifer. *The Theatre of Grotowski*. Methuen, 1985.

Leonard, George. *Mastery*. Penguin, 1992.

Leonard, George. *The Life We are Given*. GP Putnam's Sons, 1995.

Lewis, Dennis. *The Tao of Natural Breathing*. Mountain Wind Publishing, 1997.

Linklater, Kristin. *Freeing the Natural Voice*. Quite Specific Media Group, 1994.

McGough, Roger. *Sky in the Pie*. Puffin Books, 1985.

Moore, Robert. *King, Warrior, Magician, Lover*. HarperSanFrancisco, 1990.

Murray, Bill. *Second Wind*. New Theatre Publications, 2003.

Okri, Ben. *In Arcadia*. Weidenfeld & Nicolson, 2002.

Oliver, Mary. *New and Selected Poems*. Beacon Press, 1992.

Olivier, Richard. *Inspirational Leadership – Henry V and the Muse of Fire*. Spiro Press, 2001.

Oriah Mountain Dreamer. *The Invitation.* HarperSanFrancisco, 1999.

Pesso, Albert and Crandell, John. *Moving Psychotherapy.* Brookline Books, 1991.

Rodenburg, Patsy. *The Right to Speak.* Methuen, 1992.

Sher, Antony. *Year of the King.* Limelight Editions, 1992.

Stanislavsky, Constantin. *An Actor Prepares.* Methuen, 1988.

Toller, Eckhart. *The Power of Now.* Hodder & Stoughton, 2001.

Whyte, David. *Crossing the Unknown Sea.* Penguin, 2002.

Whyte, David. *The Heart Aroused.* Currency Doubleday, 1994.

Further Resources

Olivier Mythodrama – Peak Performance small group training, individual coaching and conference keynotes. Transformational leadership training, CDs and books
www.oliviermythodrama.com
Tel: +44 (0)20 7386 7972

Globe Theatre, London – see a live Shakespeare performance in the setting for which the plays were written
www.shakespeares-globe.org
Box office: + 44 (0)20 7401 9919

David Whyte – talks, tapes and books available from www.davidwhyte.com

Pesso Boyden Psychomotor System – in-depth sessions and training in dealing with inner voices
UK: www.pesso-uk.org
US and Europe: www.PBSP.com

Permissions